First World War
and Army of Occupation
War Diary
France, Belgium and Germany

48 DIVISION
144 Infantry Brigade
Gloucestershire Regiment
1/6th Battalion
29 March 1915 - 31 October 1917

WO95/2758/2

The Naval & Military Press Ltd
www.nmarchive.com
Published in association with The National Archives

Published by

The Naval & Military Press Ltd

Unit 10 Ridgewood Industrial Park,

Uckfield, East Sussex,

TN22 5QE England

Tel: +44 (0) 1825 749494

www.naval-military-press.com

www.nmarchive.com

This diary has been reprinted in facsimile from the original. Any imperfections are inevitably reproduced and the quality may fall short of modern type and cartographic standards.

© **Crown Copyright**
Images reproduced by permission of The National Archives, London, England, 2015.

Contents

Document type	Place/Title	Date From	Date To
Heading	WO95/2758/2		
Heading	48th Division 144th Infy Bde 1-6th Bn Glos Regt Apr 1915-1917 Oct		
Heading	144th Inf. Bde. 48th Div. War Diary 1/6th Battn. The Gloucestershire Regiment May (5.5.15 To 1.6.15) 1915		
War Diary	Ploegsteert	05/05/1915	11/05/1915
War Diary	Nieppe	16/05/1915	16/05/1915
War Diary	Ploegsteert	19/05/1915	27/05/1915
War Diary	Nieppe	01/06/1915	01/06/1915
Heading	144th Inf. Bde. 48th Div. Battn. Disembarked Boulogne Form England 1.4.15 War Diary 1/6th Battn. The Gloucestershire Regiment April (29.3.15-30.4.15) 1915		
War Diary	Little Baddon	29/03/1915	31/03/1915
War Diary	Boulogne	01/04/1915	01/04/1915
War Diary	Oudezeele	01/04/1915	05/04/1915
War Diary	Le Verier	05/04/1915	05/04/1915
War Diary	Armentieres	10/04/1915	10/04/1915
War Diary	Ploegsteert	17/04/1915	21/04/1915
War Diary	Pont De Nieppe	26/04/1915	26/04/1915
War Diary	Ploegsteert	30/04/1915	30/04/1915
Heading	144th Inf. Bde. 48th Div. War Diary 1/6th Battn. The Gloucestershire Regiment June 1915		
War Diary	Ploegsteert	04/06/1915	16/06/1915
War Diary	Pontdenieppe	16/06/1915	16/06/1915
War Diary	Petit Pont	19/06/1915	19/06/1915
War Diary	Messines	23/06/1915	26/06/1915
War Diary	Bailleul	27/06/1915	27/06/1915
War Diary	Vieux Berquin	27/06/1915	27/06/1915
War Diary	Robecq	28/06/1915	28/06/1915
War Diary	Burbure	29/06/1915	29/06/1915
War Diary	Trenches	01/06/1915	30/06/1915
Heading	144th Inf. Bde. 48th Div. War Diary 1/6th Battn. The Gloucestershire Regiment July (12.7.15 To 30.7.15) 1915		
War Diary	Hesdigneul	12/07/1915	12/07/1915
War Diary	Les Brebis	14/07/1915	14/07/1915
War Diary	Hurionville	17/07/1915	17/07/1915
War Diary	Lillers	19/07/1915	19/07/1915
War Diary	Mondicourt	19/07/1915	19/07/1915
War Diary	Louvencourt	19/07/1915	19/07/1915
War Diary	Bois De Warnimont	20/07/1915	20/07/1915
War Diary	Hebuterne	30/07/1915	30/07/1915
Heading	144th Inf. Bde. 48th Div. War Diary 1/6th Battn. The Gloucestershire Regiment August (8.8.15-30.8.15) 1915		
Heading	144th Inf. Bde. 48th Div. War Diary 1/6th Battn. The Gloucestershire Regiment September (5.9.15 To 17.9.15) 1915		
War Diary	Hebuterne	05/09/1915	05/09/1915
War Diary	Couin	17/09/1915	17/09/1915

Heading	144th Inf. Bde. 48th Div. War Diary 1/6th Battn. The Gloucestershire Regiment October (11.10.15-27.10.15) 1915		
War Diary	Couin	11/10/1915	11/10/1915
War Diary	Hebuterne	19/10/1915	19/10/1915
War Diary	Couin	27/10/1915	27/10/1915
Heading	144th Inf. Bde. 48th Div. War Diary 1/6th Battn. The Gloucestershire Regiment November (4.11.15-29.11.15) 1915		
War Diary	Hebuterne	04/11/1915	04/11/1915
War Diary	Couin	12/11/1915	12/11/1915
War Diary	Hebuterne	20/11/1915	20/11/1915
War Diary	Gommecourt	26/11/1915	26/11/1915
War Diary	Hebuterne	27/11/1915	28/11/1915
War Diary	Couin	28/11/1915	28/11/1915
War Diary	Couin Chateau	29/11/1915	29/11/1915
Miscellaneous	Report On Enterprise By "C" Coy. 6th Batt. Gloucestershire Regt. On Night	26/11/1915	26/11/1915
Miscellaneous	Commandant Etaples	28/12/1915	28/12/1915
Miscellaneous	Summary Of Small Offensive Operation Carried Out By 6th Battalion Gloucester Regiment (48th Division)	26/11/1915	26/11/1915
Diagram etc	Barrage For First Phase Attack Plan I		
Diagram etc	Barrage For Second Phase "Withdrawal"		
Heading	144th Inf. Bde. 48th Div. War Diary 1/6th Battn. The Gloucestershire Regiment December (2.12.15-28.12.15) 1915		
War Diary	Hebuterne	02/12/1915	06/12/1915
War Diary	Couin	14/12/1915	14/12/1915
War Diary	Hebuterne	22/12/1915	22/12/1915
War Diary	Couin	28/12/1915	28/12/1915
Heading	144th Brigade 48th Division 1/6th Battalion Gloucestershire Regiment January 1916		
War Diary	Hebuterne	03/01/1916	03/01/1916
War Diary	Couin	09/01/1916	10/01/1916
War Diary	Hebuterne	15/01/1916	15/01/1916
War Diary	Couin	21/01/1916	21/01/1916
War Diary	Hebuterne	27/01/1916	27/01/1916
War Diary	Gommecourt	30/01/1916	30/01/1916
Heading	144th Brigade 48th Division 1/6th Battalion Gloucestershire Regiment February 1916		
War Diary	Gommecourt	01/02/1916	01/02/1916
War Diary	Couin	02/02/1916	03/02/1916
War Diary	Louvencourt	03/02/1916	12/02/1916
War Diary	St Amand	12/02/1916	12/02/1916
War Diary	Hannescamps	13/02/1916	17/02/1916
War Diary	Souastre	17/02/1916	19/02/1916
War Diary	Hannescamps	21/02/1916	25/02/1916
War Diary	Bienvillers	25/02/1916	29/02/1916
War Diary	Sailly	29/02/1916	29/02/1916
Heading	144th Brigade 48th Division 1/6th Battalion Gloucestershire Regiment March 1916		
War Diary	Sailly	03/03/1916	03/03/1916
War Diary	F Sector	04/03/1916	05/03/1916
War Diary	Courcelles	06/03/1916	06/03/1916
War Diary	F Sector	07/03/1916	11/03/1916
War Diary	Courcelles	12/03/1916	12/03/1916

War Diary	F Sector	15/03/1916	19/03/1916
War Diary	Colincamps	19/03/1916	19/03/1916
War Diary	F Sector	23/03/1916	27/03/1916
War Diary	Courcelles	28/03/1916	28/03/1916
Heading	144th Brigade 48th Division 1/6th Battalion Gloucestershire Regiment April 1916		
War Diary	Courcelles	01/04/1916	01/04/1916
War Diary	F Sector	02/04/1916	03/04/1916
War Diary	Hebuterne	03/04/1916	03/04/1916
War Diary	Coigneux Sailly	08/04/1916	08/04/1916
War Diary	F Sector	14/04/1916	20/04/1916
War Diary	Couin	21/04/1916	21/04/1916
War Diary	K Sector	25/04/1916	25/04/1916
Heading	144th Brigade 48th Division 1/6th Battalion Gloucestershire Regiment May 1916		
War Diary		01/05/1916	31/05/1916
Heading	144th Brigade 48th Division 1/6th Battalion Gloucestershire Regiment June 1916		
Heading	Herewith War Diary of this Battalion for the month of June 1916.		
War Diary	J.16.d. (Sheet 57.D)	01/06/1916	01/06/1916
War Diary	Authie	01/06/1916	02/06/1916
War Diary	Gezaincourt	02/06/1916	04/06/1916
War Diary	Oneux	04/06/1916	12/06/1916
War Diary	Yvrench	12/06/1916	14/06/1916
War Diary	Outre Bois	14/06/1916	15/06/1916
War Diary	Couin	15/06/1916	21/06/1916
War Diary	J.16.d	22/06/1916	29/06/1916
Heading	144th Inf. Bde. 48th Div. War Diary 6th Battn. The Gloucestershire Regiment July 1916		
Heading	War Diary Of 6th Gloucestershire Regiment From 1st July 1916 To 31st July 1916 (Vol July 1916)		
War Diary	Sailly	01/07/1916	01/07/1916
War Diary	Mailly	02/07/1916	03/07/1916
War Diary	Serre Trenches	05/07/1916	09/07/1916
War Diary	Courcelles	09/07/1916	09/07/1916
War Diary	Serre Trenches	12/07/1916	14/07/1916
War Diary	Couin	15/07/1916	15/07/1916
War Diary	Senlis	15/07/1916	15/07/1916
War Diary	Ovillers	20/07/1916	26/07/1916
War Diary	Hedauville	27/07/1916	27/07/1916
War Diary	Arqueves	28/07/1916	28/07/1916
War Diary	Beauval	29/07/1916	29/07/1916
War Diary	Fransa	30/07/1916	30/07/1916
Miscellaneous	Appendices "A" "B" "C" "D"		
Miscellaneous	Appendix A Orders & Reports for raid attempted on July 6th 1916	06/07/1916	06/07/1916
Miscellaneous	All Companies And 8th Worcester Regiment	05/07/1916	05/07/1916
Miscellaneous	1/6th Bn. Gloucester Regiment Report On Raid On Germen Trenches	06/07/1916	06/07/1916
Miscellaneous	Appendix B Orders & Reports on Raid on night of July 13-14th 1916	14/07/1916	14/07/1916
Miscellaneous	Raid Ordered To Be Carried Out By 1/6th Gloster. Regt.	14/07/1916	14/07/1916
Miscellaneous	Report On Raid	14/07/1916	14/07/1916

Miscellaneous	Appendix C Orders & Reports on attack of the night 20/21 July 1916.	21/07/1916	21/07/1916
Operation(al) Order(s)	144th Infantry Brigade Order No. 77		
Miscellaneous	144th Infantry Brigade Amendments & Addition To Order No. 77		
Miscellaneous	1/6th Bn. Gloucestershire Regiment Supplement To War Diary	21/07/1916	21/07/1916
Miscellaneous	Appendix D Orders & Reports on attack on night of 22/23rd July 1916.	23/07/1916	23/07/1916
Operation(al) Order(s)	144th Infantry Brigade Order No. 79		
Miscellaneous	1/6th Bn. Gloucestershire Regiment Supplement To War Diary	22/07/1916	22/07/1916
Miscellaneous	H Q. 144th Inf Bde	23/07/1916	23/07/1916
Miscellaneous	H Q. 144th Inf Bde	24/07/1916	24/07/1916
Heading	144th Brigade 48th Division 1/6th Battalion Gloucestershire Regiment August 1916 Report On Operations 20th To 23rd August		
War Diary	Fransu	01/08/1916	09/08/1916
War Diary	Candas	09/08/1916	10/08/1916
War Diary	Puchevillers	10/08/1916	12/08/1916
War Diary	Bouzincourt	12/08/1916	13/08/1916
War Diary	Trenches	13/08/1916	16/08/1916
War Diary	Bouzincourt	19/08/1916	19/08/1916
War Diary	Usna Redoubt	19/08/1916	19/08/1916
War Diary	Trenches	20/08/1916	23/08/1916
War Diary	Bouzincourt	23/08/1916	26/08/1916
War Diary	Forceville	26/08/1916	26/08/1916
War Diary	Trenches	26/08/1916	27/08/1916
Miscellaneous	1/6th Bn. Gloucestershire Regt. Account Of Operations	23/08/1916	23/08/1916
Miscellaneous	1/6th Bn. Gloucestershire Regt. Account Of Operations	24/08/1916	24/08/1916
Heading	144th Brigade 48th Division 1/6th Battalion Gloucestershire Regiment September 1916		
War Diary	Thiepval	03/09/1916	03/09/1916
War Diary	Auchonvillers	06/09/1916	06/09/1916
War Diary	Bus	13/09/1916	13/09/1916
War Diary	Amplier	13/09/1916	13/09/1916
War Diary	Sarton	13/09/1916	18/09/1916
War Diary	Bois Berges	18/09/1916	30/09/1916
Heading	144th Brigade 48th Division 1/6th Battalion Gloucestershire Regiment October 1916		
War Diary	Sus-St-Leger	01/10/1916	01/10/1916
War Diary	Halloy	01/10/1916	03/10/1916
War Diary	St Amand	03/10/1916	04/10/1916
War Diary	Halloy	04/10/1916	04/10/1916
War Diary	Grenas	05/10/1916	05/10/1916
War Diary	Sailly	08/10/1916	08/10/1916
War Diary	Halloy	10/10/1916	10/10/1916
War Diary	Humbercourt	10/10/1916	13/10/1916
War Diary	St Amand	13/10/1916	13/10/1916
War Diary	Trenches	16/10/1916	19/10/1916
War Diary	St Amand	19/10/1916	20/10/1916
War Diary	Sus-St-Leger	20/10/1916	20/10/1916
War Diary	Talmas	24/10/1916	24/10/1916
War Diary	Sus-St-Leger	25/10/1916	25/10/1916
War Diary	Bresle	25/10/1916	31/10/1916
War Diary	Albert	31/10/1916	31/10/1916

Heading	144th Brigade 48th Division 1/6th Battalion Gloucestershire Regiment November 1916		
Heading	War Diary Of 1/6th Gloucester Regt. From 1st To 30th Nov. 1916 (Vol XX)		
War Diary	Albert	01/11/1916	01/11/1916
War Diary	Scott's	01/11/1916	01/11/1916
War Diary	Reserve	02/11/1916	03/11/1916
War Diary	Le Sars	05/11/1916	07/11/1916
War Diary	Scott's	08/11/1916	20/11/1916
War Diary	Eacourt L'Abayye	20/11/1916	23/11/1916
War Diary	Bazentin Wood	24/11/1916	24/11/1916
War Diary	Villa Camp	28/11/1916	28/11/1916
Heading	144th Brigade 48th Division 1/6th Battalion Gloucestershire Regiment December 1916		
War Diary	War Diary Of 1/6th Gloucestershire Regiment From 1st December 1916 To 31st December 1916 Volume 21		
War Diary	Trenches	01/12/1916	01/12/1916
War Diary	Support Trenches	05/12/1916	05/12/1916
War Diary	Shelter	05/12/1916	08/12/1916
War Diary	Trenches	09/12/1916	14/12/1916
War Diary	Shelter	15/12/1916	15/12/1916
War Diary	Mametz Wood	16/12/1916	22/12/1916
War Diary	Fricourt Camp	25/12/1916	25/12/1916
War Diary	Becourt Camp	29/12/1916	29/12/1916
War Diary	Contay	30/12/1916	30/12/1916
Heading	War Diary Of 1/6th Bn. Gloucestershire Regt From 1st To 31st January 1917 (Volume XXII)		
War Diary	Contay	06/01/1917	08/01/1917
War Diary	Heilly	08/01/1917	08/01/1917
War Diary	Pont Remy	08/01/1917	08/01/1917
War Diary	Huppy	08/01/1917	08/01/1917
War Diary	Hallencourt	22/01/1917	23/01/1917
War Diary	Huppy	26/01/1917	28/01/1917
War Diary	Oisement	28/01/1917	28/01/1917
War Diary	Warfusee	28/01/1917	28/01/1917
War Diary	Cerisy	28/01/1917	28/01/1917
Heading	War Diary Of 1/6th Bn Gloucestershire Regt. From 1st To 28th 1917 (Vol XXIII)		
War Diary	Cerisy	01/02/1917	01/02/1917
War Diary	Camp 56	02/02/1917	02/02/1917
War Diary	Herbecourt	02/02/1917	02/02/1917
War Diary	Trenches	02/02/1917	07/02/1917
War Diary	Marly	08/02/1917	08/02/1917
War Diary	Merignolles	10/02/1917	10/02/1917
War Diary	Marly	12/02/1917	17/02/1917
War Diary	G.28.b.45 (Sheet 63.c)	17/02/1917	17/02/1917
War Diary	Trenches	18/02/1917	22/02/1917
War Diary	Ravine Achille	22/02/1917	24/02/1917
War Diary	Camp 56	24/02/1917	24/02/1917
Heading	1/6th Bn. Glouc. Regt. Supplement to War Diary Feburary 1917 Appendix "A"		
Miscellaneous	1/6th Bn. Gloucestershire Regiment Supplement to War Diary February 1917	00/02/1917	00/02/1917
Heading	1/6th Bn. Gloucestershire Regiment War Diary For March 1917 Vol 24		

Type	Description	From	To
Heading	1/6th Bn Gloucestershire Regt. Supplement To War Diary March 1917 Appendix A		
Miscellaneous	1/6th Bn. Gloucestershire Regt. Supplement To War Diary March 1917 Report On Fighting Patrol	15/03/1917	15/03/1917
Heading	War Diary Of 1/6th Bn The Gloucestershire Regt. (T.F) From 1/4/17 To 30/4/17 (Vol XXIV)		
War Diary	In The Field	01/03/1917	31/03/1917
War Diary	Epehy	01/04/1917	01/04/1917
War Diary	Villars Faucon	02/04/1917	03/04/1917
War Diary	Marquaix	04/04/1917	07/04/1917
War Diary	St Emelie	08/04/1917	08/04/1917
War Diary	Out Post Line	09/04/1917	11/04/1917
War Diary	Camp At E29 G 55	12/04/1917	13/04/1917
War Diary	Marquaix	14/04/1917	16/04/1917
War Diary	Villers Faucon	17/04/1917	19/04/1917
War Diary	Out Post Line	20/04/1917	21/04/1917
War Diary	St Emelie	21/04/1917	23/04/1917
War Diary	Out Post Line	23/04/1917	25/04/1917
War Diary	Tincourt	26/04/1917	28/04/1917
War Diary	Villars Faucon	29/04/1917	29/04/1917
War Diary	Out Post Line	30/04/1917	30/04/1917
Heading	1/6th Bn. Glouc. Regt. Supplement To War Diary-April 1917 Appendix A		
Miscellaneous	1/6th Bn. Gloucestershire Regiment Battalion Operation Order	31/03/1917	31/03/1917
Miscellaneous	1/6th Bn. Gloucestershire Regiment Report On Attack On Epehy	29/04/1917	29/04/1917
Heading	1/6th Bn. Glouc. Regt. Supplement To War Diary-April 1917 Appendix "B"		
Miscellaneous	1/6th Bn. Gloucestershire Regiment Battalion Operation Order	19/04/1917	19/04/1917
Heading	1/6th Bn. Glouc. Regt. Supplement To War Diary-April 1917 Appendix "B"		
Miscellaneous	1/6th Bn. Gloucestershire Regiment Battalion Operation Order	21/04/1917	21/04/1917
Heading	1/6th Bn. Glouc. Regt. Supplement To War Diary-April 1917 Appendix "D"		
Operation(al) Order(s)	144th Infantry Brigade Order No. 173	23/04/1917	23/04/1917
Miscellaneous	144th Infantry Brigade Order No. 173	23/04/1917	23/04/1917
Miscellaneous	1/6th Bn. Gloucestershire Regiment Battalion Operation Order	23/04/1917	23/04/1917
Heading	1/6th Bn. Glouc. Regt. Supplement To War Diary April 1917 Appendix "E"		
Miscellaneous	1/6th Bn. Gloucestershire Regt. Operations Carried Out Against The "Knoll"	24/04/1917	24/04/1917
Heading	1/6th Bn. Glouc. Regt. Supplement To War Diary-April 1917 Operation Order No. 1		
Miscellaneous	1/6th Bn. Gloucestershire Regiment Battalion Operation Order No. 1	29/04/1917	29/04/1917
Miscellaneous	Reference Battalion Operation Order No. 1	29/04/1917	29/04/1917
Heading	War Diary Of 1/6th Bn. The Gloucestershire Regt. 1st May To 31st May 1917 (Vol XXVI)		
War Diary	Outpost Line	01/05/1917	02/05/1917
War Diary	Villars Faucon	03/05/1917	04/05/1917
War Diary	Buire	05/05/1917	10/05/1917
War Diary	Peronne	11/05/1917	12/05/1917

Type	Description	Start	End
War Diary	Combles	13/05/1917	13/05/1917
War Diary	Fremicourt	14/05/1917	21/05/1917
War Diary	Trenches Near Morchies	22/05/1917	29/05/1917
War Diary	Beavmetz-Morchies Line	30/05/1917	31/05/1917
Operation(al) Order(s)	1/6th Bn. Gloucester Regt. Battn. Operation Order No. 2	01/05/1917	01/05/1917
Operation(al) Order(s)	1/6th Bn. Gloucestershire Regiment Battalion Operation Order No. 3	03/05/1917	03/05/1917
Operation(al) Order(s)	1/6th Bn. Gloucestershire Regiment Battalion Operation Order No. 4	11/05/1917	11/05/1917
Operation(al) Order(s)	1/6th Bn. Gloucestershire Regiment Battalion Operation Order No. 5	12/05/1917	12/05/1917
Operation(al) Order(s)	1/6th Bn. Gloucestershire Regiment Battalion Operation Order No. 6	13/05/1917	13/05/1917
Operation(al) Order(s)	1/6th Bn. Gloucestershire Regiment Battalion Operation Order No. 7	22/05/1917	22/05/1917
Operation(al) Order(s)	1/6th Bn. Gloucestershire Regiment Battalion Operation Order No. 8	30/05/1917	30/05/1917
Heading	War Diary Of 1/6th Bn The Gloucestershire Regt. (T.F) 1st June To 30th June 1917 (Vol XXVII)		
War Diary	Morchies	01/06/1917	05/06/1917
War Diary	Trenches	06/06/1917	14/06/1917
War Diary	Fremicourt	15/06/1917	22/06/1917
War Diary	Trenches	23/06/1917	30/06/1917
Operation(al) Order(s)	1/6th Bn. Gloucestershire Regiment Battalion Operation Order No. 9	05/06/1917	05/06/1917
Operation(al) Order(s)	1/6th Bn. Gloucestershire Regt. Battalion Operation Order No. 10	14/06/1917	14/06/1917
Operation(al) Order(s)	1/6th Bn. Gloucestershire Regiment Battalion Operation Order No. 11	17/06/1917	17/06/1917
Operation(al) Order(s)	1/6th Bn. Gloucestershire Regiment Battalion Operation Order No. 12	23/06/1917	23/06/1917
Heading	War Diary Of 1/6th Bn. Gloucestershire Regt. (T.F) 1st July To 31st July 1917 (Vol XXVIII)		
War Diary	Trenches	01/07/1917	02/07/1917
War Diary	Beugny	03/07/1917	03/07/1917
War Diary	Achiet-Le-Petit	04/07/1917	04/07/1917
War Diary	Hendecourt	05/07/1917	20/07/1917
War Diary	Bienvillers	21/07/1917	22/07/1917
War Diary	Poperinghe	23/07/1917	23/07/1917
War Diary	St Jans-Ter-Biezen	24/07/1917	31/07/1917
Operation(al) Order(s)	1/6th Bn. Gloucestershire Regiment Battalion Operation Order No. 14	07/07/1917	07/07/1917
Operation(al) Order(s)	1/6th Bn. Gloucestershire Regiment Battalion Operation Order No. 15	03/07/1917	03/07/1917
Operation(al) Order(s)	1/6th Bn. Gloucestershire Regiment Divisional Tactical Exercise Operation Order No. 16	15/07/1917	15/07/1917
Operation(al) Order(s)	1/6th Bn. Gloucestershire Regiment Battalion Operation Order No. 17	20/07/1917	20/07/1917
Operation(al) Order(s)	All Coys T.O H.Q. Mch O.O. No. 18	21/07/1917	21/07/1917
Operation(al) Order(s)	1/6th Bn. Gloucestershire Regiment Battalion Operation Order No. 19	30/07/1917	30/07/1917
Heading	War Diary Of 1/6th Bn. The Gloucestershire Regt. (T.F.) From 1/8/17 To 31/8/17 (Vol XXIX)		
War Diary	Camp A.29 D	01/08/1917	06/08/1917
War Diary	Dambre Camp	07/08/1917	08/08/1917

War Diary	Trenches	09/08/1917	13/08/1917
War Diary	In Support	14/08/1917	15/08/1917
War Diary	Reigersberg	16/08/1917	16/08/1917
War Diary	Canal Bank	17/08/1917	17/08/1917
War Diary	In Support	18/08/1917	20/08/1917
War Diary	Front Trenches	21/08/1917	23/08/1917
War Diary	Canal Bank	24/08/1917	24/08/1917
War Diary	Reigersberg	25/08/1917	26/08/1917
War Diary	In Support	27/08/1917	28/08/1917
War Diary	Dambre Camp	29/08/1917	29/08/1917
War Diary	St. Jan-Ter-Biezen	30/08/1917	31/08/1917
Operation(al) Order(s)	1/6th Bn. Gloucestershire Regiment Battalion Operation Order No. 20	05/08/1917	05/08/1917
Operation(al) Order(s)	1/6th Bn. Gloucestershire Regiment Battalion Operation Order No. 21	08/08/1917	08/08/1917
Operation(al) Order(s)	1/6th Bn. Gloucestershire Regiment Battalion Operation Order No. 22	10/08/1917	10/08/1917
Operation(al) Order(s)	1/6th Bn. Gloucestershire Regiment Battalion Operation Order No. 24	13/08/1917	13/08/1917
Operation(al) Order(s)	1/6th Bn. Gloucestershire Regiment Battalion Operation Order No. 23	11/08/1917	11/08/1917
Operation(al) Order(s)	1/6th Bn. Gloucestershire Regt. Battalion Operation Order No. 25	17/08/1917	17/08/1917
Operation(al) Order(s)	1/6th Bn. Gloucestershire Regiment Battalion Operation Order No. 26	18/08/1917	18/08/1917
Operation(al) Order(s)	1/6th Bn. Gloucestershire Regiment Battalion Operation Order No. 27	20/08/1917	20/08/1917
Operation(al) Order(s)	1/6th Bn. Gloucestershire Regiment Battalion Operation Order No. 28	22/08/1917	22/08/1917
Miscellaneous	1/6th Bn. Gloucestershire Regiment Appendix To Battalion Operation Order No. 28	21/08/1917	21/08/1917
Operation(al) Order(s)	1/6th Bn. Gloucestershire Regiment Battalion Operation Order No. 29	23/08/1917	23/08/1917
Operation(al) Order(s)	1/6th Bn. Gloucestershire Regiment Battalion Operation Order No. 30	24/08/1917	24/08/1917
Operation(al) Order(s)	1/6th Bn. Gloucestershire Regiment Battalion Operation Order No. 31	28/08/1917	28/08/1917
Heading	War Diary Of 1/6th Bn. The Gloucestershire Regiment T.F. From 1/9/17 To 30/9/17 (Vol XXX)		
War Diary	St Jan-Ter-Biezen	01/09/1917	17/09/1917
War Diary	Zutkerque	18/09/1917	30/09/1917
Operation(al) Order(s)	1/6th Bn. Gloucestershire Regiment Battalion Operation Order No. 32	16/09/1917	16/09/1917
Operation(al) Order(s)	1/6th Bn. Gloucestershire Regt. Battalion Operation Order No. 33	27/09/1917	27/09/1917
Miscellaneous	Artillery Barrage		
Operation(al) Order(s)	1/6th Battalion Gloucestershire Regiment Battalion Operation Order No. 34	30/09/1917	30/09/1917
Heading	1/6th Gloucestershire Regiment War Diary 1st October-31st October 1917 Volume XXXI		
War Diary	Zutkerque	01/10/1917	01/10/1917
War Diary	Vlamertinghe Brake Camp	02/10/1917	04/10/1917
War Diary	Canal Bank	05/10/1917	05/10/1917
War Diary	Dambre Camp	06/10/1917	07/10/1917
War Diary	Irish Fm	07/10/1917	07/10/1917
War Diary	Dambre Camp	08/10/1917	08/10/1917

War Diary	Trenches	09/10/1917	10/10/1917
War Diary	Siege Camp	11/10/1917	12/10/1917
War Diary	St Janter Biezen	13/10/1917	13/10/1917
War Diary	Tinques	14/10/1917	15/10/1917
War Diary	Villers Au Bois	16/10/1917	17/10/1917
War Diary	Vimy	18/10/1917	21/10/1917
War Diary	Front Line	22/10/1917	24/10/1917
War Diary	Trenches	25/10/1917	25/10/1917
War Diary	Neuville St Vaast	26/10/1917	31/10/1917
Operation(al) Order(s)	Operation Orders No. 34a By Lt. Col. H. St. G. Schomberg, Comdg. 1/6th Bn Gloucestershire Regt.	04/10/1917	04/10/1917
Operation(al) Order(s)	Operation Orders No. 34b By Lt Col H. St. G. Schomberg Comdg 1/6th Bn Gloucestershire Regt	04/10/1917	04/10/1917
Operation(al) Order(s)	1/6th Bn. Gloucestershire Regiment Battalion Operation Order No. 35	06/10/1917	06/10/1917
Operation(al) Order(s)	Operation Order No. 35a by Lt Col H. St. G. Schomberg Comdg 1/6th Bn Gloucestershire Regt	07/10/1917	07/10/1917
Operation(al) Order(s)	Operation Order No. 36 by Lt Col H. St. G. Schomberg Comdg 1/6th Bn Gloucestershire Regt	08/10/1917	08/10/1917
Operation(al) Order(s)	Operation Order No. 37 by Lt Col H. St. G. Schomberg Comdg 1/6th Bn Gloucestershire Regt	08/10/1917	08/10/1917
Miscellaneous	Report On Attack By 1/6th Bn. Gloucestershire Regt. On Morning	09/10/1917	09/10/1917
Operation(al) Order(s)	Operation Order No. 42 by Lt Col H. St. G. Schomberg Comdg 1/6th Bn Gloucestershire Regt	25/10/1917	25/10/1917

WO/95/2758/2

1/6 Battalion Gloucestershire Regiment

48TH DIVISION
144TH INFY BDE

1-6TH BN GLOS REGT
APR 1915-MAR 1919

1917 OCT

TO 1 THLY

144th Inf.Bde.
48th Div.

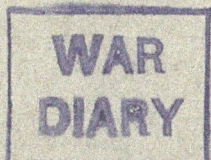

1/6th BATTN. THE GLOUCESTERSHIRE REGIMENT.

M A Y

(5.5.15 to 1.6.15)

1 9 1 5

Army Form C. 2118.

WAR DIARY
or
INTELLIGENCE SUMMARY.
(Erase heading not required.)

Instructions regarding War Diaries and Intelligence Summaries are contained in F.S. Regs., Part II. and the Staff Manual respectively. Title pages will be prepared in manuscript.

Hour, Date, Place	Summary of Events and Information	Remarks and references to Appendices
11.55 pm May 5th PLOEGSTEERT	to Bde reserve. Took over trenches from 4th Glosters.	
11.2 am 7/5/15 "	"	
12.55 am 16/5/15 NIEPPE	to Divisional reserve.	
11.15 pm 19/5/15 PLOEGSTEERT	Took over trenches from 4th Glosters.	
11.45 am 23/5/15 "	to Bde Reserve	
9.30 pm 27/5/15 "	Took over trenches from 4th Glosters.	
12.28 am 1/6/15 NIEPPE	to Divisional reserve	
	During May the weather, with the exception of one week, has been good. Strength the Batt. — 3 officers and 118 other ranks (below establishment). Casualties Officers 1 killed and 1 wounded. Other ranks 14 " 45 " " 14 " "	

J. Micklem. Lt. Col.
1/6 Gloster Regt.

144th Inf.Bde.
48th Div.

Battn. disembarked
Boulogne from
England 1.4.15.

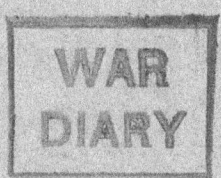

1/6th BATTN. THE GLOUCESTERSHIRE REGIMENT.

A P R I L

(29.3.15-30.4.15)

1 9 1 5

Army Form C. 2118.

WAR DIARY
or
INTELLIGENCE SUMMARY.
(Erase heading not required.)

Hour, Date, Place	Summary of Events and Information	Remarks and references to Appendices
1.30 A.M. 29/3/15 LITTLE BADDOW	Transport & 84 men left under Lts. BIRD & LAXTON.	
1.15 P.M. 31/3/15 "	Batt. less transport paraded to move.	
12.45 A.M. 1/4/15 BOULOGNE	Batt. arrived.	
10. P.M. 1/4/15 OUDEZEELE	Batt. went into billets.	
8. A.M. 5/4/15 LE VERIER	Batt. paraded to move.	
2.30 P.M. 5/4/15 "	Batt. arrived.	
5.30 P.M. 10/4/15 ARMENTIERES	Batt. arrived to be attached to 17th Inf Bde for instruction.	
7. P.M. 17/4/15 PLOEGSTEERT	Batt. in Bde Reserve.	
7.30 P.M. 21/4/15 "	Took over Right Section of Bde line.	
8. A.M. 25/4/15 PONT DE NIEPPE	Went into billets in Divisional Reserve having been relieved by 4th Glosters.	
11. P.M. 30/4/15 PLOEGSTEERT	Took over centre from 4th Glosters.	
	During April the weather has been very good. Strength of Batt. is 1 Officer (2nd Lt ANDERSON) and 61 other Ranks below establishment. Casualties Officers Nil. Other Ranks 4 killed 13 wounded	

J. Micklem Capt
A/Capt 1/6 Gloucesters Regt

144th Inf.Bde.
48th Div.

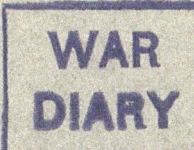

1/6th BATTN. THE GLOUCESTERSHIRE REGIMENT.

J U N E

1 9 1 5

WAR DIARY
or
INTELLIGENCE SUMMARY.

(Erase heading not required.)

Army Form C. 2118.

Instructions regarding War Diaries and Intelligence Summaries are contained in F.S. Regs., Part II. and the Staff Manual respectively. Title pages will be prepared in manuscript.

Hour, Date, Place			Summary of Events and Information	Remarks and references to Appendices
10–5 pm	June 4	PLOEGSTEERT	Took over trenches from 4th Gloster	During the month of June the weather was great with the exception of the last week which has wet.
8.30 pm	9/6/15	"	In Bde reserve	
7–10 pm	13/6/15	"	Took over trenches from 4th Gloster	
9.30 pm	15/6/15	"	Handed over trenches to 5th, 7th & 8th Warwicks	
1–5 am	16/6/15	PONT DE NIEPPE	In Divisional Reserve	Strength of Batln is 3 Officers and 139 other ranks below establishment.
7.50 pm	19/6/15	KPETIT PONT	In Bde Reserve	Casualties—Officers nil Other ranks killed 4 wounded 14
11.15 pm	20/6/15	MESSINES	Took over trenches from 4th Gloster	
10.30 pm	25/6/15	"	Handed over trenches to 4th Royal Fusiliers	
11.50 pm	26/6/15	"	Handed over trenches to Kensington & 5th & 7th Canadians	
4.30 am	27/6/15	K BAILLEUL	Arrived in billets	
11.40 am	"	VIEUX BERQUIN	arrived in billets	
10.5 am	28/6/15	ROBECQ	arrived in billets	
9–15 pm	29/6/15	BURBURE	arrived in billets	

F.K. Newbold
Lt Col 1/6 Gloster Regt

Army Form C. 2118.

WAR DIARY
or
INTELLIGENCE SUMMARY.

(Erase heading not required.)

Instructions regarding War Diaries and Intelligence Summaries are contained in F. S. Regs., Part II. and the Staff Manual respectively. Title pages will be prepared in manuscript.

Place	Date	Hour	Summary of Events and Information	Remarks and references to Appendices
TRENCHES	10th to 5th June		In the Trenches Section 4. No incident of note. Total casualties during this tour of duty 5 (all wounded)	
	6th		Bn Brigade Reserve at H.20.a.d. Working parties made new communication trenches to No 4 Section of considerable length.	
	11th Jun		Took over trenches No 4 Section from 7th Bn West Riding Reg't at 8 p.m.	
	11th Jun to 12th		Nothing of note occurred.	
	13th	5 p.m.	Took over 5 P. and 5 Q. of Section 5. Quiet all day.	
	14th		French Mortars were in use most of the day both by the enemy and ourselves. Pte. S. Harris and Pte. Bailey killed. Pte. Bellamy wounded (bullet).	
	15th	2 a.m.	Pte Sampson wounded while with working party in front of trenches. Working party making new communication trench to No 4 Section. Pte Knight slightly wounded in shoulder.	
	16th		2nd Lieut Coulter killed. Pte Anthony 'B' Coy ——— killed. Pte S. Labourne 'A' Coy severely wounded.	
	17th		Nothing of note occurred on this date.	
		8.30 p.m.	7th Battalion took over No 4 Section. Latrines accounted for by 2 Taubes hovering over Headquarters for a long period.	
	18th to 23rd		Divisional Reserve at H.20.o.d. Working parties on new communication trenches and forts both day & night.	
	23rd	7.30 p.m.	Took over trenches No 4 Section from 7th West Riding Regt.	

INTELLIGENCE SUMMARY

(Erase heading not required.)

Place	Date	Hour	Summary of Events and Information	Remarks and references to Appendices
TRENCHES	24th Jan.	3 a.m.	Pt. Fisher of 'A' Coy killed while out with wire party; buried at 11 a.m. Enemy working parties active; moving down ground in front of parapet, and strengthening parapet. Machine Gun turned on them, but with what effect not known. Very quiet during day.	
		9 p.m.	Working party of 7th Battalion improved & began new bays of new support trench.	
	25th		L/cpl Birkett T. 'C' Coy. killed whilst out with wire party early morning; buried opposite Headquarters at 11 a.m. Orders received to move SOUTH. Spare baggage sent away at 3 p.m.	
	26th.		In trenches. Relieved by Rifle Brigade 12 midnight.	
	27th	3.30 a.m.	Reached billets near SCIAZY. About 7 mile march.	
		5 a.m.	Marched to DOULIEU, about 6 miles. Went into bivouac in orchard.	
		9 p.m.	Saw two Canadian Brigades marching north.	
	28th.		Still in bivouac. Returned Maps to Brigade. Though wretched by companies after equipment, boots, and special inspection and attention to feet.	
	29th.	8 p.m.	Brigade marched from DOULIEU to FLETRE, arriving about 10 p.m. Battalion billeted in large farm; the best billet the Battalion has experienced. Distance of march about 9 miles.	
	30.	8 p.m.	Brigade marched at 8 p.m. from FLETRE arriving ST JANS-TER-BIEZEN. about 2 a.m. Distance about 13 miles. Owing to prolonged trench work the Battalion soft & some twenty fell out. Whole Brigade billeted in large wood.	

144th Inf.Bde.
48th Div.

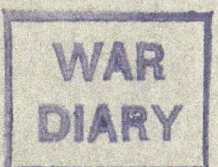

1/6th BATTN. THE GLOUCESTERSHIRE REGIMENT.

J U L Y
(12.7.15 to 30.7.15)
1 9 1 5

Army Form C. 2118.

WAR DIARY
or
INTELLIGENCE SUMMARY.
(Erase heading not required.)

Instructions regarding War Diaries and Intelligence Summaries are contained in F.S. Regs., Part II. and the Staff Manual respectively. Title pages will be prepared in manuscript.

Hour, Date, Place	Summary of Events and Information	Remarks and references to Appendices
11.10 pm July 12th MESDIGNEUL	Went into Bivouac.	During the month of July the weather was variable.
1.30 AM " 14th LES BREBIS	Arrived in billets.	Strength of this Batt. is 7 Officers below & 9 other ranks over establishment
3.45 AM 17th HURIONVILLE	Arrived in billets.	Casualties during the month
6.30 AM 19th LILLERS	Entrained.	Killed nil.
1.0 pm " MONDICOURT	Detrained.	3 Other Ranks wounded.
4.45 pm " LOUVENCOURT	Arrived in billets.	
4.30 pm 20th BOIS DE WARNIMONT	Went into bivouac.	
11.30 pm 30th HEBUTERNE	Took over trenches from 5th WARWICKS.	

L. C. Nott Lt.
Act Adjt
1/6 E Glouc Regt

(73989) W4141—463. 400,000. 9/14. H.&J.Ltd. Forms/C. 2118/10.

144th Inf.Bde.
48th Div.

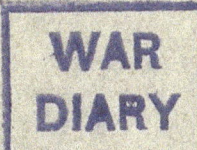

1/6th BATTN. THE GLOUCESTERSHIRE REGIMENT.

A U G U S T

(8.8.15-30.8.15)

1 9 1 5

144th Inf.Bde.
48th Div.

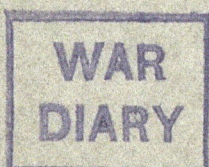

1/6th BATTN. THE GLOUCESTERSHIRE REGIMENT.

S E P T E M B E R

(5.9.15 to 17.9.15)

1 9 1 5

WAR DIARY
or
INTELLIGENCE SUMMARY. 1/6th Batt Glouc. Regt.
(Erase heading not required.)

Hour, Date, Place	Summary of Events and Information	Remarks and references to Appendices
6.0 pm 5/9/15 HEBUTERNE	Took over K Sector HEBUTERNE trenches from Bucks Batt.	
9.20 pm 17/9/15 COUIN	Went into Divisional Reserve.	
	During September the weather was mostly fine. Strength of Batt. is 1 officer over & 17 O.R. under establishment. Casualties. O.R. 1 killed. 2 wounded.	

J. C. Pott Lt a/adjt
1/6th Glouc. Regt.

1/10/15.

144th Inf.Bde.
48th Div.

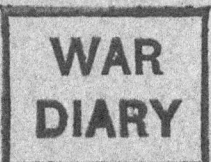

1/6th BATTN. THE GLOUCESTERSHIRE REGIMENT.

O C T O B E R

(11.10.15 - 27.10.15)

1 9 1 5

WAR DIARY or INTELLIGENCE SUMMARY.

(Erase heading not required.)

Army Form C. 2118.

1/6th Glouc. Regt.

Hour, Date, Place	Summary of Events and Information	Remarks and references to Appendices
7.0 pm 11/10/15	COUIN went into Div. Res.	
2.45 pm 19/10/15	HEBUTERNE Took over K Sector trenches from BUCKS Battn.	
	19th – 27th 5th 8th G.R. just involves attached for instruction	
5.45 pm 27/10/15	COUIN went into Div. Res.	
	During October the weather was very unsettled, misty, dull & wet. Strength of Battn. is 2 officers over and 4 O.R. over establishment.	
	Casualties. O.R. 1 officer accidentally wounded 1. O.R. killed 2. O.R. wounded.	

S.C. Nott Lt/adjt
1/6th Glouc. Regt.

1/11/15.

144th Inf.Bde.
48th Div.

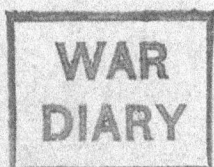

1/6th BATTN. THE GLOUCESTERSHIRE REGIMENT.

N O V E M B E R

(4.11.15 - 29.11.25)

1 9 1 5

Attached:

Report on Operation
on Night of 25th/
26th November.

Army Form C. 2118.

WAR DIARY
or
INTELLIGENCE SUMMARY.
(Erase heading not required.)

1/6th Glouc. Regt.

Hour, Date, Place	Summary of Events and Information	Remarks and references to Appendices
3.5 p.m. Nov. 4th HEBUTERNE.	Took over K. Sector trenches from Bucks Battn. On our left 5th or 6th Battn. R. Warwick Regt. On our right 4th Battn. Gloucs Regt. B Coy 13th R. Irish Rifles attached front	
5.20 p.m. Nov 12th COUIN.	Went in Div. Res.	
2.30 p.m. Nov 20th HEBUTERNE	Took over K Sector trenches from Bucks Battn. On our left 5th or 6th R. Warwicks. On our right 4th Gloucs. B Coy 13th R. Irish. Rifles attached from 20th to 25th. C Coy make surprise attack on corner of Gommecourt Wood, supported by 3rd S.M. RFA Bde. Full account attached.	
1.3 a.m. Nov 26th GOMMECOURT		
11.30 p.m. Nov 27th — 3.30 a.m. — 28th HEBUTERNE	Enemy shelled us during night, and kept up bursts of rapid fire. Appeared very nervous.	
2.15 p.m. Nov 28th COUIN	Went into Div Reserve.	
2.30 p.m. Nov 29th COUIN chateau.	Inspected by Corps Commander. VII Corps.	
	During November. Weather was fairly severe. Heavy Rain. Snow + frosts. Strength of Battn. to 1 officer and 24 OR under establishment. Casualties. Capt. P.G. IRVINE {died of wounds. 2nd Lts BADGELEY + PRYCE wounded. Lt C.E. SCHWALM killed in action. 2 OR missing. 23 OR wounded.	L C Mott Lt adjt 1/6th Glouc Regt.

(73989) W4141-463. 400,000. 9/14. H.&J.Ltd. Forms/C. 2118/10.

Report on enterprise by "C" Coy. 6th Batt. Gloucestershire
Regt. on night of 25th / 26th November 1915.

S C H E M E.

To raid the German trenches and shelters at K.4.c.8.6.
(S.E. Corner of GOMMECOURT WOOD) and obtain prisoners and
information as to trenches, garrison, etc. Strong works are
known to exist at this point.

Strength of party, five officers, 100 other ranks. Of
these, two parties of 25, each under an Officer, told off to
enter trenches at X and Y on attached plan I. Remaining 3
Officers and 50 other ranks to be in support in "Z" hedge at W on
plan I. As soon as the two parties are in position 70 yards
from German trenches, "ready" to be signalled back to Artillery
who commence first barrage, as shewn on plan I. The object of
this barrage is to make the German sentries take cover, drown
the noise of our party approaching, and cutting the wire, and
subsequently to prevent German reinforcements coming up from the
second line. The first gun to be the signal for the assaulting
parties to rush. Bombing parties to be left at each communication
trench and the remainder of the two assaulting parties to work to
the central point and then retire on to the support. The whole
party then to retire to our trenches and second barrage (see
plan II) to open to cover retirement.

A preliminary bombardment by Artillery to take place
on the afternoon of the 25th to cut the wire, damage trenches,
and attract a working party from whom prisoners are likely to be
obtained. The Infantry rehearsed the scheme on a similar portion
of our trench very carefully, both by day and night.

E X E C U T I O N.

Preliminary bombardment, successfully executed by
Artillery, at 4-40 p.m. on 25th.

At 11-35 p.m. 90 men of "C" Coy. 6th Gloucestershire
Regt. under Capt. V.L.Young, left their trenches and reached the
"Z" hedge, joining the garrison consisting of Lieut. H.P.Mott and
20 other ranks who had been there since dark to prevent the
Germans occupying it and to keep off any hostile patrols.

The two parties of 25 each, under 2/Lieut. P.P.PRYCE
and 2/Lieut. J.E.C.Badgeley, respectively, moved off at 12-00 am.
Owing to bright moonlight they had to move very slowly and
reached position of readiness 70 yards from German trench at
12-40 am.

Capt. Young received reports by telephone at 12-52 am.
that they were ready to assault.

He waited for a cloud to cover the moon before asking
advanced R.A. Officer for No. 1 barrage. At 1-1 am. the signal
"ready" was sent back to the Artillery who opened fire at 1-3 am.
and both parties rushed.

L E F T   P A R T Y.
(2/Lieut. J.E.C.Badgeley)

This party cut through two wire entanglements, the second
one being very low, strong, thick wire, 5 yards deep. The
unavoidable noise and delay caused by this gave the enemy sentries
the alarm. 2/Lieut. Badgeley and 10 men got into the trench.
2/Lieut. Badgeley shot two men and the first dug-out was bombed
with two bombs. The enemy retired then along the trench to left
and twelve bombs were thrown at our party, from the parallel in
rear.

Touch was gained with the right party, but Lieut.
Badgeley was wounded by a bomb which fell at his feet. This party
then retired, bringing in all their wounded; one of the latter
was killed on the way back by a chance bullet.

RIGHT PARTY.
(2/Lieut. T.T. Pryce).

This party only found low wire and entered the German trench without alarming the enemy. The first shelter was a telephone office; one German was just coming up the steps and was called upon to surrender. As he did not do so Lieut. Pryce shot him and the shelter was then bombed with three bombs. A blocking party was established and the N.C.O. in charge pulled up a sump cover which effectually prevented the German supports from reaching our party. Led by Lieut. Pryce they proceeded down the trench and bombed six shelters in succession. They took 3 unarmed German prisoners; as these were being passed down the trench for evacuation, they darted into a shelter, reappeared armed, and attacked our party in the rear. They were all killed. Lieut. Pryce having lost touch with left party, began his retirement up the trench, but found it full of Germans who had apparently reinforced from underground passages. Our party bombed this crowded trench most successfully, climbed out of the trench and retired with all their wounded. The Germans pursued, but were driven back by bombs. Lieut. Pryce had previously been slightly wounded by a pistol bullet from a German Officer, whom he killed with his revolver. The party safely reached hedge, with the exception of one man who had been sent back with a message to the signallers and was never subsequently seen. One wounded prisoner was brought in by this party.

WITHDRAWAL.

Capt. Young, having collected the whole of the party at the "Z" hedge, telephoned to the R.A. to stop first barrage, and sent his men back to the trenches in small parties, by pre-arranged routes. Lieut. D.H.Hartog, with rifle grenade party, moved off to the left and enfiladed the enemy's trench, which was presumably crowded, with twelve rifle grenades. The whole party returned without further casualties.

Killed - 1 man. Missing - 1 man.
Wounded - 2/Lieut. J.M.C.Badgeley.
          2/Lieut. T.T.Pryce.
          18 other ranks.

All the wounded are slight cases, and five are at duty.

The raid was most successful, and must have accounted for a large number of Germans, who were caught crowded in big, deep shelters and bombed.

From the prisoner's statement, the garrison at present in the trench was A Company 180 strong. Eight Germans were killed in the trench outside the shelters.

The success of the enterprise was due to the bravery and keenness of both men and officers, and to the careful previous rehearsing and organization of the parties, full advantage being taken of the information which has been collected and circulated after former attacks.

Composition, formation and equipment of Storming Parties.

Each assaulting column was formed as under:-
  Officer.
  4 men with rifles and fixed bayonets.
  4 men, each carrying 12 bombs, bludgeon, and bayonet as dagger.
  4 men, each with bludgeon and bayonet as dagger.
  4 men, with revolvers and bayonets as daggers (for escort to prisoners).
  4 men, with rifles and fixed bayonets.
  4 men, with 12 bombs each, bludgeon and bayonet as dagger (these last two sections of fours detailed to block and hold communication trench and point of entry.
  2 telephone men, with instrument, to remain at point of entry.

Support Party at "Z" hedge.

3 Officers.
6 Grenadiers with rifle grenades.
60 men in fighting order, with rifles, bayonets, and
   reserve of bombs.
1 Officer R.F.A. with telephone and operator.
3 Telephone operators for Infantry with 3 instruments.

Communications.   Both Artillery and Infantry had separate new
                   telephone lines, laid from Artillery O.P. in our
                   trenches to support at "Z" hedge. Each assaulting
                   party took a telephone and two operators forward
                   with lines back to two separate instruments at
                   "Z" hedge. Instruments for assaulting party were
                   specially tuned down to buzz quietly. Communic-
                   ations worked perfectly and touch was never lost.

Bombs.   Amount carried, as detailed on previous page,
                   all No. 5. They were all new and freshly detonated:
                   none failed to explode. Grenades were difficult
                   to throw so as to reach the bottom of the deep
                   shelters without lodging on the steps. Some of our
                   men were wounded by splinters from our own bombs.
                   Bombs containing heavy gas would have absolutely
                   prevented the enemy from reinforcing through deep
                   shelters and underground tunnels as they did.

Condition of   Very good condition, revetted with rabbit wire and
German trenches.   stakes. About 10 feet deep, firing bays for
                   5 men each, with good steps leading up to them.
                   Trenches in chalk, but not boarded or bricked, with
                   large sump holes. Shelters very deep, some with
                   spiral staircases. All appeared to be connected by
                   underground passages to each other and back to
                   second line. Large traverses 8 or 9 feet broad.
                   The high wire that was encountered was good, but
                   where only low wire was encountered i.e. to the
                   right, it offered no obstacle. The Germans appear
                   to have some method of pulling up a single strand
                   of wire as this was set by our party on leaving
                   the trenches, though it was not there when they
                   went in.
                   A few specially prepared rifle pits were found
                   just outside the parapet, 4' square and 4' deep.
                   The trenches appeared practically undamaged by our
                   Artillery bombardment of the previous afternoon.

Report of action of 3rd S.M.F.A. Brigade in support of 8th Batt.
Gloucestershire Regt. on night 20th/26th November 1915.

   An Artillery Officer with a Signaller accompanied the
Company Commander with the "Z" hedge and was in touch with
the R.A. Commander throughout the operations.
   The word "ready" was received and fire on lines of first
barrage, open at rate of section fire five seconds, at 1-3am
   At request of Infantry Company Commander, at "Z" hedge,
this quick rate was kept up till 1-10 am, then slowed down
to section fire 20 seconds, and at 1-12 am, to section fire
30 seconds. At 1-13 am, "Stop" was received from forward
officer and barrage ceased.
   At 1-14 am, second barrage asked for by R.A. F.O.O.
under orders of the Company Commander. This message was
received through both Artillery and Infantry telephones
and order sent to the Battery, but almost immediately
"stop" was received from the F.O.O. and transmitted to
Battery.
   At 1-20 am, first barrage again asked for and opened.
This was kept up until 1-30 am, when "stop" was received.

Artillery stood by ready to open second barrage, but this was not asked for and at 2 am. Infantry reported "All in".

The barrage seemed to be well maintained and effective. Telephone communication between F.O.O. and Brigade Commander and through By. Ors. to Batteries worked without a hitch. No. of rounds fired throughout the operations by 3 Batteries - 340 Shrapnel.

Retaliation by enemy's Artillery was slight and rather dilatory and was mostly directed at our front trenches. Fifty to sixty rounds from Field Guns from direction of LA LOUVIERE and howitzers from direction of Bois du BIEZ were fired into section "X" between 1-30 am. and 2 am.

                (Signed) A.R.B.COSSART Lt. Col.
                              R.A.
           Comdg. 3rd S.M.F.A. Brigade.

26th Nov. 1915.

              To accompany Plans I and II.

Two sketches to illustrate barrages of fire by 3rd South Midland F.A. Brigade to support parties of 6th Batt. Gloucestershire Regiment.

1st Phase.

    An R.A. Officer and signaller will accompany the Infantry Company Commander to the "Z" hedge and be in communication with R.A. Brigade Commander. As soon as Infantry send back word that the two parties are ready to rush in, the Artillery will open fire, forming the barrage of the 1st Phase.

    A quick rate of fire will be maintained for the first 30 seconds, after which a slower rate of fire will be kept up on the same line, till information is received that the Infantry have got back to the "Z" hedge.

2nd Phase.

    The barrage of the second phase would be formed if and when the Infantry require it.

                (Signed) A.R.B.COSSART Lieut. Col.
           Comdg. 3rd. S.M.F.A. Brigade.

SECRET.

G.S./350.

Commandant
Etaples

    The attached copy of a minor operation carried out on 25/26th November 1915 is forwarded in continuation of my memorandum of yesterday.

H.Q., I.G.C.
28/12/15.

R. McDonald
Lieutenant-Colonel,
G.S.

48th Division

SECRET.

Summary of small offensive operation carried out
by 6th Battalion Gloucester Regiment (48th Division),
on 25th/26th November 1915.

1. Object of operation.

   (a) To cause loss to the enemy and reduce his moral.

   (b) To obtain information as to enemy's trenches and to secure prisoners.

2. Previous training.

Thorough reconnaissances of the ground over which the attack was to proceed were made. *The infantry rehearsed the scheme on a similar portion of our trenches very carefully by day & by night.*

3. Scheme.

Strength of party, five officers, 100 other ranks. Of these, two parties of 25, each under an officer, told off to enter trenches at X and Y on attached plan I. Remaining 3 officers and 50 other ranks to be in support in "Z" hedge at W on plan I. As soon as the two parties are in position 70 yards from German trenches, "ready" to be signalled back to Artillery who commence first barrage, as shown on plan I. The object of this barrage is to make the German sentries take cover, drown the noise of our party approaching, and cutting the wire, and subsequently to prevent German reinforcements coming up from the second line. The first gun to be the signal for the assaulting parties to rush. Bombing parties to be left at each communication trench and the remainder of the two assaulting parties to work to the central point and then retire on to the support. The whole party then to retire to our trenches and second barrage (see plan II) to open to cover retirement

A preliminary bombardment by Artillery to take place on the afternoon of the 25th to cut the wire, damage trenches, and attract a working party from whom prisoners are likely to be obtained.

4. __Execution.__

Preliminary bombardment, successfully executed by Artillery at 2-40 p.m. on 25th.

At 11-35 p.m. 90 men of "C" Company, 6th Gloucestershire Regiment under Captain V.L.Young, left their trenches and reached the "Z" hedge, joining the garrison consisting of Lieutenant H.P.Nott and 20 other ranks who had been there since dark to prevent the Germans occupying it and to keep off any hostile patrols.

The two parties of 25 each, under 2/Lieutenant T.T.Pryce and 2/Lieutenant J.M.C.Badgeley, respectively, moved off at 12-20 a.m. Owing to bright moonlight they had to move very slowly and reached position of readiness 70 yards from German trench at 12-45 a.m.

Captain Young received reports by telephone at 12-58 a.m. that they were ready to assault.

He waited for a cloud to cover the moon before asking advanced R.A.Officer for No.1 barrage. At 1-1 a.m. the signal "ready" was sent back to the Artillery who opened fire at 1-3 a.m. and both parties rushed.

5. __Left Party.__   (2/Lieutenant J.M.C.Badgeley).

This party cut through two wire entanglements, the second one being very new, strong, thick wire, 5 yards deep. The unavoidable noise and delay caused by this gave the enemy sentries the alarm. 2/Lieutenant Badgeley and 10 men got into the trench, 2/Lieutenant Badgeley shot two men and the first dug-out was bombed with two bombs. The enemy retired then along the trench to left and twelve bombs were thrown at our party, from the parallel in rear.

Touch was gained with the right party, but Lieutenant Badgeley was wounded by a bomb which fell at his feet. This party then retired, bringing in all their wounded; one of the latter was killed on the way back by a chance bullet.

5. __Right Party.__   (2/Lieutenant T.T.Pryce).

This party only found low wire and entered the German trench without alarming the enemy. The first shelter was a telephone office; one German was just coming up the steps and was called upon to

surrender

surrender. As he did not do so Lieutenant Pryce shot him and the shelter was then bombed with three bombs. A blocking party was established and the N.C.O. in charge pulled up a sump cover which effectually prevented the German supports from reaching our party. Led by Lieut Pryce they proceeded down the trench and bombed six shelters in succession. They took 3 unarmed German prisoners; as these were being passed down the trench for evacuation, they darted into a shelter, re-appearing armed, and attacked our party in the rear. They were all killed. Lieut Pryce, having lost touch with left party, began his retirement up the trench, but found it full of Germans who had apparently reinforced from underground passages. Our party bombed this crowded trench most successfully, climbed out of the trench and retired with all their wounded. The Germans pursued, but were driven back by bombs. Lieut Pryce had previously been slightly wounded by a pistol bullet from a German Officer, whom he killed with his revolver. The party safely reached hedge, with the exception of one man who had been sent back with a message to the signallers and was never subsequently seen. One wounded prisoner was brought in by this party.

7. Withdrawal.

Captain Young, having collected the whole of the party at the "Z" hedge, telephoned to the R.A. to stop first barrage, and sent his man back to the trenches in small parties, by prearranged routes. Lieut. D.H. Hartog, with rifle grenade party, moved off to the left, and enfiladed the enemy's trench, which was presumably crowded, with twelve rifle grenades, with twelve rifle grenades. The whole party returned withour further casualties.

8. Result of operation.

The raid was most successful, and must have accounted for a large number of Germans, who were caught crowded in big, deep shelters and bombed.

From the prisoner's statement, the garrison at present in the trench was a company 180 strong, of 169th Regt. 8 Germans were
killed...

killed in the trench outside the shelters.

The success of the enterprise was due to the bravery and keenness of both men and Officers, and to the careful rehearsing and organization of the parties, full advantage being taken of the information which has been collected and circulated after former attacks.

9. <u>Casualties</u>.

    Killed - 1 man, missing - 1 man.

    Wounded - 2/Lieut. J.M.C.Badgeley
                2/Lieut T.T. Pryce
                18 other ranks.

All the wounded are slight cases, and five are at duty.

10. <u>Composition, formation and equipment of storming parties.</u>

Each assaulting column was formed as under :-

            ŏ   Officer

ŏ ŏ ŏ ŏ   4 men with rifles and fixed bayonets

ŏ ŏ ŏ ŏ   4 man, each carrying 12 bombs, bludgeon, and bayonet as dagger.

ŏ ŏ ŏ ŏ   4 men, each with bludgeon and bayonet as dagger.

ŏ ŏ ŏ ŏ   4 men with revolvers and bayonets as daggers (for escort to prisoners).

ŏ ŏ ŏ ŏ   4 men, with rifles and fixed bayonets.

ŏ ŏ ŏ ŏ   4 men, with 12 bombs each, bludgeon, and bayonet (these last two sections of fours detailed to block and hold communication trench and point of entry)

    ŏ ŏ   2 telephone men, with instrument, to remain at point of entry.

Support party at "Z" hedge.

    3 Officers.
    6 Grenadiers with rifle grenades.
  50 men in fighting order, with rifles, bayonets, and reserve of bombs.
    1 Officer, R.F.A. with telephone and operator.
    3 telephone operators for infantry with three instruments.

11 Communications.

Both artillery and infantry had separate new telephone lines, laid from artillery O.P. in our trenches to support at "Z" hedge. Each assaulting party took a telephone and two operators forward, with lines back to two separate instruments at "Z" hedge. Instruments for assaulting party were specially tuned down to buzz quietly. Communications worked perfectly and touch was never lost.

12 Bombs

Amount carried as detailed on previous page, all No.5. They were all new and freshly detonated. None failed to explode. Grenades were difficult to throw so as to reach the bottom of the deep shelters without lodging on the steps. Some of our men were wounded by splinters from our own bombs. Bombs containing heavy gas would have absolutely prevented the enemy from reinforcing through deep shelters and underground tunnels as they did.

13. Action of Artillery (3rd S.Midland F.A. Brigade.)

An artillery Officer with a signaller accompanied the Company Commander to the "Z" hedge and was in touch with the R.A. Commander throughout the operations.

The word "ready" was received and the fire on lines of first barrage, open at the rate of section fire five seconds, at 1-3 a.m.

At request of infantry company Commander, at "Z" hedge, this quick rate was kept up till 1-10 a.m./ then slowed down to section fire 30 seconds, and at 1-12 a.m. to section fire 30 seconds. At 1-13 a.m. "stop" was received from forward officer and barrage ceased.

At 1-14 a.m. second barrage asked for by R.A. F.O.O. under orders of the Company Commander. This message was received through both artillery and infantry telephones and order sent to the Battery, but almost immediately "Stop" was received from the F.O.O. and transmitted to Battery.

At 1-20 a.m.

At 1-20 a.m. first barrage again asked for and opened. This was kept up till 1-29 a.m. when "stop" was received.

Artillery stood by ready to open second barrage, but this was not asked for and at 2 a.m. infantry reported "all in".

The barrage seemed to be well maintained and effective. Telephone communication between F.O.O. and Brigade Commander and through Battery Commanders to Batteries worked without a hitch. No. of rounds fired throughout the operations by 3 Batteries :- 340 shrapnel.

Retaliation by enemy's artillery was slight and rather dilatory and was mostly directed at our front trenches. Fifty to sixty rounds from Field Guns from direction of LA LOUVIERE and howitzers from direction of BOIS du BIEZ were fired into section "K" between 1-30 a.m. and 2 a.m..

14- Artillery barrages.

1st phase.

An R.A. Officer and signaller will accompany the infantry company commander to the "Z" hedge and be in communication with R.A. Brigade Commander.

As soon as Infantry send back word that the two parties are ready to rush in, the artillery will open fire, forming the barrage of the 1st phase.

A quick rate of fire will be maintained for the first 30 seconds, after which a slower rate of fire will be kept up on the same line, till information is received that the infantry have got back to the "Z" hedge.

2nd phase.

The barrage of the 2nd phase would be formed if and when the infantry require it.

Barrage for First Phase "Attack"

PLAN I

2nd Battery (4 Guns)
N⁰ˢ 4, 3, 2 and 1

Gommecourt Wood

1st Battery (2 Guns)
N⁰ˢ 4 and 3

"Z" hedge

Telephone

O.P.F.
Bde
Comdr
O.P.G.

HEBUTERNE

Front Line of Sector "K"

3rd Battery (1 Gun)
N⁰ 4

REFERENCE
① Barrage for First Phase "Attack"
— German Trench.

Barrage for Second Phase "Withdrawal"

PLAN II

1 Battery (4 Guns)
Nos 4, 3, 2 and 1

O.P.F.
Bde Comdr
O.P.C.

Front Trench Sector "K"

REFERENCE
① Barrage for Second Phase "Withdrawal"
— German Trenches.

144th Inf.Bde.
48th Div.

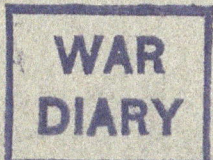

1/6th BATTN. THE GLOUCESTERSHIRE REGIMENT.

D E C E M B E R

(2.12.15 - 28.12.15)

1 9 1 5

Army Form C. 2118.

WAR DIARY
or
INTELLIGENCE SUMMARY.
(Erase heading not required.)

1/6th Glouc. Regt.

Hour, Date, Place	Summary of Events and Information	Remarks and references to Appendices
Dec. 2. HEBUTERNE.	Draught of 50 O.R. arrived from 3rd Entrenching Battn.	
3.30 p.m. " 6. HEBUTERNE.	Took over K Sector trenches from Bucks Battn. On our left 5t or 6t Battn. R.Warwick Regt. On our right 1/4t Battn. Glouc. Regt.	
5.45 p.m. " 14. COUIN.	Went in Div. Res: 1/6t Manchester Regt. attached from 6–14t Dec.	
3.30 p.m. " 22. HEBUTERNE.	Took over K Sector trenches from Bucks Bttn. On our left 5t or 6t Battn. R.Warwick Regt. On our right 1/4t Battn. Glouc. Regt. 1/8t King's L'pool Regt. attached from 22nd–24th Dec.	
7 p.m. " 28. COUIN.	Went in Div. Res:	
	During December weather was fairly severe. Heavy rain. Strength of Battn. 10 + 4 officers sick, (wages nursing) + 5 O.R. over establishment. Casualties. Lt. D.H. Hartog to England sick 22 Dec. 2 O.R. Killed in action. 3 O.R. died of wounds. 7 O.R. wounded. 2nd Lt. C.H. Carruthers. gazetted 29/10/15. 2nd Lt. J. Fletcher joined for duty 24/12/15 from 1st Entr. Battn.	

McK[ ] [signature]
1/1/16

[signature]
1/1/16

144th Brigade.
48th Division.

1/6th BATTALION

GLOUCESTERSHIRE REGIMENT

JANUARY 1 9 1 6

Army Form C. 2118.

WAR DIARY
or
INTELLIGENCE SUMMARY.
(Erase heading not required.)

1/4th Bn. Gloucester Regt.
January 1916

Hour, Date, Place	Summary of Events and Information	Remarks and references to Appendices
2.30pm Jan 3rd HEBUTERNE	Took over K Sector HEBUTERNE defences from Bucks Battalion	Vol 17/10
5.30pm Jan 9th COUIN	to Div. Reserve billets	Took over K sector when relieved
10am Jan 10th COUIN	G.O.C. in C. B.E.F. rode through village	3.O.R. wounded
5.30pm Jan 16th HEBUTERNE	Took over K Sector HEBUTERNE defences from Bucks Battalion	4th Gloucesters R.H.
6.0pm Jan 21st COUIN	Went into Div. Reserve billets. Were relieved in trenches by 4th OXFORD & BUCKS LI.	
11.0pm Jan 27th HEBUTERNE	Took over "K" sector from 4th OXFORDS	
4am Jan 30th GOMMECOURT	A raid on enemy trenches at S.W. corner of the new a the PARC DE GOMMECOURT was attempted, but owing to fog parties had to return to our lines. Own casualties slight. Enemy having the matter known the enemy very quiet.	
	Casualties 1 O.R. Killed 5 O.R. Wounded	
	Strength of Battn. in officers up to establishment 22 O.R. not at strength.	
	2nd Lt. HOLMAN seconded to signal school Lt. ANDERSON " " " " 2nd Lt. DURANT to 1/4th Bn. Durham L.I. Capt. FULLERTON	L.Clark Capt. Adjt. for O.C. 1/4th Glouc.

10P

144th Brigade.

48th Division.

1/6th BATTALION

GLOUCESTERSHIRE REGIMENT

FEBRUARY 1 9 1 6

Army Form C. 2118.

WAR DIARY
or
INTELLIGENCE SUMMARY.
(Erase heading not required.)

1/6TH GLOUC. REGT.

Hour, Date, Place	Summary of Events and Information	Remarks and references to Appendices
10.15 p.m. Feb 1st GOMMECOURT.	Successful Bombing attack carried out by 2nd LT RUGMAN and 10 NCO's & men on enemy Y Sap at K.3.d.7.5 (sheet 57.D)	During the first fortnight of February the weather was changeable & wet. From 15th-18th it was very stormy & wet. From the 19th it was very cold with some fall of snow.
5.15 p.m. Feb 2nd COUIN.	Div Res billets.	
9.15 a.m. " 3rd COUIN	Left COUIN for LOUVENCOURT.	
12.20 p.m. " 3 LOUVENCOURT.	In billets.	
2.15 p.m. " 12th LOUVENCOURT.	Left for ST AMAND.	CASUALTIES
6.15 p.m. " 12th ST AMAND	All in billets.	Officers. 1 wounded
7.45 p.m. " 13th HANNESCAMPS.	Took over trenches from E.5C.63 to E.16.d.54 (sheet 57.D note 142). Helys near HANNESCAMPS CHURCH. Took over from 11 R.WARWICKS & from 2 Coy 6 K BEDFORDS	O.R. 1 killed 6 wounded.
8.0 p.m. Feb 13. HANNESCAMPS	Relief complete 7.50 p.m.	Strength of Batt. in trow. 5 officers in the 12 K Bde. 2 Strength. 1100.R. over.
7.0 p.m. Feb 17th "	Were relieved in trenches by 4th Glouc.	Reinforcement 119 O.R joined on Feb 20th 205.
8.45 p.m. " 17th SOUASTRE	In Div Res. billets. (Enemy raid on 7.Worc)	LT H. HELLIER OH through R. 17F.
6.30 p.m. " 14th "	Stood to for 2 hrs owing to bomb attack on 12 K Bde.	2nd LT G.B. MONTAGUE joined for duty on 165.
6.0 p.m. " 21 HANNESCAMPS.	Relived 4th Glouc in P Sector trenches.	
6.45 p.m. " 25th "	Were relieved by 4th Glouc.	
7.30 p.m. " 25 BIENVILLERS.	In Bde Reserve Billets.	
4.0 p.m. " 29 "	Left for SAILLY	
7.30 p.m. " 29 SAILLY	All in billets.	

J.M.E.H Ly Lt Col
1/3/16

144th Brigade.
48th Division.

1/6th BATTALION

GLOUCESTERSHIRE REGIMENT

MARCH 1 9 1 6

WAR DIARY or INTELLIGENCE SUMMARY

1/6th GLOUC REGT. Army Form C. 2118.

(Erase heading not required.)

Hour, Date, Place			Summary of Events and Information	Remarks and references to Appendices
5.30 pm	March 3rd	SAILLY	Left billets for trenches.	
1.15 am	" 4th	F5 Sector	Took over trenches from 2nd ESSEX. 12th BDE	
11.35 pm	" 5th	F5 Sector	Were relieved by 4th Glouc.	
2.45 am	" 6th	COURCELLES	In Divisional Res. billets.	
10.0 pm	" 7th	F5 Sector	Took over trenches from 4th Glouc.	
			1 Composite Coy resting in billets at SAILLY.	
9.50 pm	" 11th	F5 Sector	Were relieved by 4th Glouc.	
12.5 am	" 12th	COURCELLES	In Div. Res. billets.	
10.50 pm	" 15th	F5 Sector	Relieved 4th Glouc.	
2.0 am	" 19th	"	Enemy bombarded very heavily line at K23d.5.7	
			(Sheet 57.D parts 3 +4) barraged front line, support lines	
			and Communication trenches to left of sector.	
			Our artillery opened barrage at 2.3 am.	
2.15 am	" 19th	"	Gas. lachrymatory, and smoke shells sent over.	
2.20 am (about)	" 19th	"	Enemy raided 3 posts at K.23.d.95.75, K.23d.48	
			and K.23.d.35.95. Carrying off 3 men. Out of 24 men	
			holding these 3 posts. 10 were killed. 3 wounded, 3 missing.	
2.20 am	" 19th	"	Platoon from support line ordered to Counterattack.	
2.25 am	" 19th	"	Posts reoccupied. 1 Personnel (unwounded) captured. of B. Coy. 66th Regt.	
2.50 am	" 19th	"	Enemy ceased firing.	
3.0 am	" 19th	"	All quiet. Total Casualties due to raid	
			12 killed. 1 off (2 Lt J.G. HOLMAN) gassed.	
			29 O.R. wounded or gassed (3 of which died of wounds)	

Army Form C. 2118.

WAR DIARY
or
INTELLIGENCE SUMMARY.
(Erase heading not required.)

Hour, Date, Place	Summary of Events and Information	Remarks and references to Appendices
9.35 p.m. March 19th. F Sector.	Relieved by 4th Glouc.	Strength of Battalion is now 5 officers & 102 O.R. over strength.
11.20 p.m. "	COLINCAMPS. In Bde. Res. billets.	
11.30 p.m. 23rd F Sector.	Took over trenches from 4th Glouc.	Reinforcements during March. 2nd Lt D.F. HARRIS. 10th 2nd Lt R.G. TITLEY. 11th 2nd Lt S.S. HARRIS. 19th 17 O.R. on 19th 50 O.R. on 21st. Capt. H.E.H. SUTTON posted 2nd Lt on 12th
10.0 p.m. 27th F Sector.	Relieved by 4th Glouc.	
12.25 A.m. 28th COURCELLES.	In Div. Res. billets.	
	During February the weather was extremely severe from the 5th – 11th and was very changeable during the whole month.	
	Casualties. 2nd Lt G. BRINDAL } wounded. 18th Capt V.L. YOUNG. } 2nd Lt J.G. HOLMAN. gassed. 19th	
	O.R. Killed 19. Wounded 44 (3 of which died of wounds) Missing 4. Died 1.	M Marling Major Comg 1/6th Glouc. Regt.

144th Brigade½
48th Division.

1/6th BATTALION

GLOUCESTERSHIRE REGIMENT

APRIL 1 9 1 6

WAR DIARY
or
INTELLIGENCE SUMMARY.

1/6th GLOUC. REGT.

Army Form C. 2118.

Hour, Date, Place	Summary of Events and Information	Remarks and references to Appendices
Apl. 1st COURCELLES	In Div. RESERVE hutts.	
10.45pm " 2nd F Sector	Relieved 4th GLOUC.	
4.30pm " 3rd do	Gave over ½ F Sector to 1/4th YORKS & LANCS. 9/4th BDE. Have now held from K.29.b.1.9 to K.23.b.1.5. (Bdy. 5/d paris 3+4) 2 Coys moved back to billets.	
4.30pm " 5th HEBUTERNE	Relieved by 4th GLOUC. 2 Coys in huts COIGNEUX. 2 Coys in billets SAILLY, in BDE RESERVE.	
10.35pm " 8th COIGNEUX SAILLY		
7pm " 14th F Sector	Relieved 4th GLOUC.	
9pm " 20th do	Relieved by 1/6th W. YORKS from LUKE COPSE to NAIRN ST incl. & WRANGLE. NAIRN ST excl. to WRANGLE.	Strength of Battalion 7 officers under strength 110 O.R.
12.30pm " 21st COUIN	Moved to hutments COUIN. In DIV. RESERVE.	
2.30pm " 25th K Sector	Relieved 1/4th OXFORD & BUCKS.	

Weather very fine during April, with exception of period between 21st & 25th which was wet.

Casualties. LT H.P. NOTT. killed in action 27th Apl.
LT. COL. I. MICKLEM. Struck off strength 24th Apl.
CAPT. H.H. KAXTON do 25th "
O.R. Wounded 9.

O.R. 26. on 8th Apl.
O.R. 21 " 14th "
O.R. 34 " 29th "

Reinforcements. LT. I.M. FOWLIE. joined for duty 14th Apl.

M Farlane Major
cmdg 1/6 Glouc. Regt.

144th Brigade.
48th Division.

1/6th BATTALION

GLOUCESTERSHIRE REGIMENT

MAY 1916

Copy / XLVIII 149

1HR
5 sheets

WAR DIARY

Army Form C. 2118.

Instructions regarding War Diaries and Intelligence Summaries are contained in F.S. Regs., Part II and the Staff Manual respectively. Title pages will be prepared in manuscript.

INTELLIGENCE SUMMARY.

16th Bn. Gloucestershire Regiment
May 1916

(Erase heading not required.)

Hour, Date, Place	Summary of Events and Information	Remarks and references to Appendices
May 1st	In trenches. K Sector HEBUTERNE.	
2nd	Relieved by 1st Bucks Battalion, and moved back to huts at COIGNEUX.	
3rd	In huts.	
4th	Brigade march to BEAUVAL starting 5 a.m. Battalion all in billets 10 a.m. Corps Commander Lt General Sir Aylmer Hunter-Weston inspected Brigade at MARIEUX.	
5th	In billets. Company training.	
6th	-do-	
7th	-do-	
8th	-do-	
9th	-do-	
10th	-do-	
11th	-do-	
12th	-do-	
13th	-do-	
14th	-do-	
15th	Left BEAUVAL at 6 a.m. for COUIN. Very wet march. Brigade at COUIN. All in 10.45 a.m.	
16th	Relieved Bucks Battalion in H Sector, HEBUTERNE. Relief complete 5.15 pm. (continued)	

Army Form C. 2118.

WAR DIARY (Contd.) 1/6th Bn. Gloucestershire Regiment.
or
INTELLIGENCE SUMMARY. May 1916.

(Erase heading not required.)

Hour, Date, Place	Summary of Events and Information	Remarks and references to Appendices
May 17th	In trenches.	
18th	-do-	
19th	-do-	
20th	-do-	
21st	-do-	
22nd	-do-	
23rd	-do-	
24th	Relieved by 4th Glouc Regt. and proceeded to bivouacs at SAILLY DELL. J.16.d.	
25th	In bivouacs	
26th	-do-	
27th	-do-	
28th	-do-	
29th	-do-	
30th	-do-	
31st	-do-	
	Casualties during month.	
	Wounded 3 other ranks.	
	Died of Wounds 1 other rank.	
	R.S.Ferguson Lieut & Adjt.	
	for 1/6 16th Bn. Gloucestershire Regt.	

144th Brigade.

48th Division.

1/6th BATTALION

GLOUCESTERSHIRE REGIMENT

JUNE 1916

Secret.

D.A.G.,
3rd. ECHELON.

Herewith War Diary of this Battalion

for the month of June 1916.

[signature] Nicholson
Lt.Col.
Comdg. 1/6th Bn. Gloucestershire Regiment

1/7/16.

1/6th Glouc. Regt. June
C.E. 15

Army Form C. 2118.

WAR DIARY
or
INTELLIGENCE SUMMARY.
(Erase heading not required.)

June 1916.

Hour, Date, Place	Summary of Events and Information	Remarks and references to Appendices
11.0 am J.16.D. (Sheet 57.A) June 1st	Left bivouacs. marched to AUTHIE. Arrived	
1.0 pm AUTHIE June 1st	Left in billets.	
6.0 am AUTHIE June 2nd	Left Billets. Bde March	
10.0 am GEZAINCOURT June 2nd	In billets.	
9.0 am GEZAINCOURT June 4th	Left Billets. Training on ST RIQUIER. 30ff & 1800 OR on June 5th	
1.0 pm ONEUX "	In billets. Training were sent to AMIENS on a working party	
10.0 pm ONEUX June 12th	Left billets. 2off & 90 OR sent on working party to PUCHEVILLERS	
12.30 pm YVRENCH June 12th	Arrived in billets.	
1.0 pm YVRENCH June 14th	Left Billets. In billets. 70 men returned from AMIENS. 30ff & 200 OR sent to MONTRELET and BERNUEIL	
7.30 pm OUTRE BOIS "	In bivouacs.	
5.0 am OUTRE BOIS June 16th	Left billets. 2off & 90 OR sent to RAINCHEVAL. 10ff & 52 sent to Amplier	
12.30 pm COVIN "	In bivouacs. 3 off & 220 sent to GEZAINCOURT.	
8.0 pm COVIN June 21st & 22nd	Parties from RAINCHEVAL: & GEZAINCOURT returned.	
12 noon June 22nd "	moved to billets in J.16.d. Another party of 1 off & 100 OR sent to RAINCHEVAL	
12 noon June 24th "	Parties from AMIENS, MONTRELET & BERNUEIL. reported.	
4.0 pm June 28th "	Party from RAINCHEVAL (2 off 200R) reported	
3.0 am June 29th "	Party from PUCHVILLERS Reported	
	During June the weather was very changeable. Casualties Nil. Strength of Battn officers 9 under strength. O.R. 60 under strength	

J.C. 15 R
1st Bat.
B.L. McCalmont Lt-Col
Comndg 1/6 Gloster

144th Inf.Bde.
48th Div.

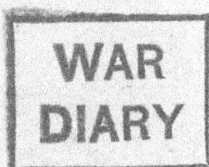

6th BATTN. THE GLOUCESTERSHIRE REGIMENT.

J U L Y

1 9 1 6

Attached:

Appendices "A", "B", "C" & "D".

CONFIDENTIAL.

WAR DIARY.

OF

6th GLOUCESTERSHIRE REGIMENT.

FROM 1st JULY, 1916 to 31st JULY, 1916.

(VOL: JULY, 1916).

Army Form C. 2118.

1/6th GLOUC REGT.

WAR DIARY
or
INTELLIGENCE SUMMARY.
(Erase heading not required.)

Instructions regarding War Diaries and Intelligence Summaries are contained in F. S. Regs., Part II. and the Staff Manual respectively. Title pages will be prepared in manuscript.

Place	Date	Hour	Summary of Events and Information	Remarks and references to Appendices
SAILLY	1st	8.0 pm	Left bivouacs at T.16.d. near SAILLY & moved to bivouacs on W side of MAILLY. Held in reserve there all day. LIEUTS. PARAMORE. BLAD, T LOMAN, and 2nd LTS. FOWLE BARRINGTON. BALDERSON. CORBETT. T STOVELL of the Devonshire Regt joined for duty.	
MAILLY	2nd	8.0 pm	Under orders to attack enemy Trenches N of River ANCRE and opposite MARY REDAN. Left bivouacs & marched to forming up position. Attack was ordered for 3.15 am but was cancelled at 12.30 am just as we were forming up.	
MAILLY	3rd	4.0 am	Arrived back in bivouacs.	
MAILLY	3rd	5.0 pm	Left MAILLY. Marched back to SAILLY bivouacs. All in.	
SERRE Trenches	5th	12.30 am	Relief of F Sector complete. Took over from 94th Bde. Had orders to attack German front & second line opposite MARK & MATTHEW Copses at 2.30 am. Attack postponed 24 hrs & then cancelled.	
"	6th	1.30 am	B Coy attempted a raid. Report see Appendix A.	A.
"	7th		Capt. BIRD. LIEUT. TUCKER. 2nd LTS FLETCHER. MONTAGUE & FOWLE wounded.	
"	9th	12.0 m	Relieved by 4th Glouc.	
COURCELLES	9th	3.15 am	In billets. D Coy mess shelled. 2 men stewards wounded. Lt FOWLIE to Hospital.	
SERRE Trenches	12th	11.30 am	Took over F sector.	
"	13th	12.15 am	In conjunction with other operations. D Coy raided. Report Appendix B.	B.
"	14th	3.25 am	Let off a Smoke Cloud for 20 mins.	

Army Form C. 2118.

WAR DIARY
or
INTELLIGENCE SUMMARY.
(Erase heading not required.)

Instructions regarding War Diaries and Intelligence Summaries are contained in F. S. Regs., Part II. and the Staff Manual respectively. Title pages will be prepared in manuscript.

Place	Date	Hour	Summary of Events and Information	Remarks and references to Appendices
SERRE Trenches	14th	8.0 pm	Were relieved by 11th S.W. Borderers. Went into bivouac on S. side of Couin - St Leger Road.	
COUIN	15th	1.0 pm	Left bivouac in motor busses.	
SENLIS	15th	2.0 pm	In bivouac at V.23.6.55 Sheet 57.d.SE.	
"	"	8.0 pm	Left bivouac marched through BOUZINCOURT - S. of MARTINSART - AVELOY - Reserve Trenches at W.18.b Sheet 57.d.SE. HQ DONNET POST.	
OVILLERS	20th	3.0 pm	Relieved 4th Glouc on line points 37.66.02.26 & 47. Arilleri spec.T.M.	C
"	21st	2.30 am	Attacks made on points 39. 88. 28 2.0, & 62. Reports Appendix.	
"	22nd	4.0 pm	Relieved by 4th Glouc. moved back to trenches round DONNET post.	
"	23rd	12.30 am	Enemy line & fort between points 90. & 40. attacked. Reports Appendix	D
"	23rd	10.0 am	Remnants of Batt back in trenches round DONNET POST.	
"	24th		Draft of 129 OR. 8. 8th were officers temporarily attached.	
"	26th	4.0 pm	Relieved by 6th Buffs. Went into billets at BOUZINCOURT in 6.30 pm.	
HEDAUVILLE	27th	4.10 pm	Leaving BOUZINCOURT at 2.15 pm. In billets bivouac HEDAUVILLE.	
ARQUEVES	28th	10.30 am	Leaving HEDAUVILLE at 7.15 am. In billets ARQUEVES.	
BEAUVAL	29th	10.30 am	Leaving ARQUEVES at 7.15 am. Arrived in billets at BEAUVAL.	
FRANSU	30th	10.30 am	Leaving BEAUVAL at 3.45 am. Arrived in billets at FRANSU.	

WAR DIARY
INTELLIGENCE SUMMARY

1/6th Glouc. Regt.

Army Form C. 2118.

Place	Date	Hour	Summary of Events and Information	Remarks and references to Appendices
			The weather during July was on the whole very fine + hot from the 1st - 9th June. 4th - 8th showery. 8th - 24th Fair. 24th to end of the month very fine. Casualties during month.	

Killed. Officers. Capt. G.E. ELLIOTT. MAJ. C.E. COATES. LIEUT. R.E. PARAMORE (Devon Regt)
2/7/16   23/7/16

2nd Lt S.H. CORBETT. T G.C. DILLON.
(Devon Regt)   23/7/16

Missing. 8.K 2nd Lt. H.P. BALDERSON (Devon Regt)

Died of Wounds. 2nd Lt A.R. SMITH and Capt. E.W. BIRD.
                    22/7/16   (27/7/16)

Wounded. Lieuts. [H.E.] TUCKER. W.H. ANDERSON. 2nd Lts J.A. FLETCHER
                    [7/7/16]   (23/7/16)   (7/7/16)

CAPT. MONTAGUE and A FOWLE (Devon Regt)   C.H. CARRUTHERS. M. DURANT.
(7/7/16)   (3/7/16) attached 99   23/7/16

L.A.H. STOVELL (Devon Regt) and H.E. HICKSUTTON. L. SCULL.
23/7/16   attached   21/7/16   24/7/16

Gassed. 2nd Lt W. COOMBS.

O.R. Killed. 15. missing 62. Wounded. 296. Died of wds. 5.
believed killed 20

Strength of Batt - is now below strength
+ 162 O.R. below strength.   8 Officers of the 8 Devon Regt
were attached to Batt provisionally on the 24/7/16. + are still attached.
LIEUTS. H.A. WILMOT, A.R. CLARE SMITH and A.G. POOLE joined
for duty from 15th Glouc. on 30/7/16.

APPENDICES

"A"
"B"
"C"
"D"

Appendix A.

Orders & Reports for
raid attempted on July 6th
1916.

ALL COMPANIES AND 8th WORCESTER REGIMENT.

"B" Coy. will raid enemy's first and second line at 1-30 a.m. tomorrow (6th inst.) morning.

They will start from front line trench between MATTHEW and MARK COPSES and try to penetrate at roughly K.29.b.30.40. and K.29.b.15.15.

There will be no barrage and no increase of rifle and M.G. fire but ordinary fire will be maintained on the flanks of the raiding parties. In the event of the parties becoming heavily engaged a barrage will be started and rifle and M.G. fire opened on the German front trenches on the flanks to keep down hostile rifle fire. The signal for opening heavy rifle and M.G. fire will be the starting of the barrage.

The raiding parties will wear pieces of white bandage tied to their shoulder straps. Their pass-word is OLD MARKET and if challenged on returning to our trenches they will answer OLD MARKET.

July 5th 1916.

Lieut. Col.
Comdg. 1/6th Gloucester Regiment.

1/6th Bn. Gloucester Regiment.

REPORT ON RAID ON GERMAN TRENCHES. JULY 6th 1916.

Two parties, each a platoon strong, under Second Lieuts. FULLERTON and SMITH left our front line at 1-30 am, right party intending to penetrate German Line at K.29.b.15.15 and left party at K.29.b.30.40.

As left party reached a point about the centre of the remains of the German front line wire a sentry fired two shots. Orders were then heard to be shouted in the German trench and a very large number of bombs were thrown out.

It was estimated by several independent observers that bombs were being thrown on a front of 250 yards by Bombers not more than five yards apart on the whole front.

One member of the left party penetrated the German trench. He was wounded and information collected from him will be forwarded later. This party threw six bombs.

Right party were slower than the left party and had not reached the German wire when the enemy started throwing bombs hard in front of them. A certain amount of rifle fire and fire from two machine guns was opened while the bombs were being thrown.

The raiding party consider that enemy was lined out behind parados.

About ten minutes after the bombs started to be thrown one large Minenwerfer and several Mortars opened fire on our front line also some Field Gun shells and a few 4.2's. About twelve 4.2's fell between Battalion Headquarters and Observation Wood.

Watching from Battalion Observation Station, the German line appeared to be strongly held and well organised.

As soon as the bombs started to be thrown, continuous flares were fired from the flanks, as if this has been previously arranged.

A large number of coloured rockets were fired. Details of these will be forwarded later.

I do not consider that parties of the strength sent out could possibly have penetrated the German line in the face of the resistance offered.

The whole of the raiding parties got in with seven wounded.

During the shelling, one man was killed and two wounded in the front trench and six wounded in the neighbourhood of OBSERVATION WOOD.

6/7/16.

Lieut. Col.
Comdg. 1/6th Bn. Gloucester Regt.

Appendix. B.

Orders &
Reports on Raid
on night of July 13-14th
1916

Raid ordered to be carried out by
1/6th Gloster Regt.
on night 13/14 July 1916

Object. To penetrate enemy's front line and to take prisoners. Specimens of enemy to be brought in alive or dead, particularly any suspected of being gas casualties due to 4th Div. emission previous to raid.

Point to be raided. Large portions of the enemy front line are known to be derelict and not held. Enemy is known to hold his line at K.29.b.2.3 as sentries can always be seen at this point. This portion of enemy line to be cut out and cleared.

Formation. 2 officers and 45 men, one officer leading and one officer in rear.
Strength

To move in fours.

Leading officer and 30 men to 'cross' enemy trench at Southern corner of enemy strong point, then to wheel to left along back of enemy trench. When they are behind the portion of trench selected they are to turn towards home, drop into enemy trench, clear it, bomb the shelters and then return to our line. These 30 men to consist of 10 bayonet men in fatigue dress with rifle and fixed bayonet and 20 bombers carrying 6 (no 5) grenades each (in pockets) and bayonet or bludgeon.

Remaining officer and 15 men to remain at point of entry. Bombing group of 1 (?) bayonet men and 4 bombers to move 15ˣ down enemy trench to right to prevent any attempt to bomb

92

up from the flank. Remaining 9 men to remain at point of entry to take over prisoners and form small reserve of bombs. This party will consist in all of 1 Officer, 6 bayonet men in fatigue dress with rifle and fixed bayonet and 9 bombers with bag of 10 (No 5) grenades each and bayonet or bludgeon.

Time. This raiding party will be found by D Company and will be in first line between MATTHEW and MARK COPSES ready to move off at any moment after 11. P.M 3¼.

Code for telephone. Raiders have left our trenches.
APPLE.
Raiders have returned to our trenches
PEACH.
Raid success.
STRAWBERRY

Code
(cont)

Raid failure
　　　MEDLAR.

Prisoners unwounded
　　　PLUM (with numeral
to denote number secured)

Prisoners wounded.
　　　CHERRY (with numeral)

Enemy corpses brought in
　　　BANANA (with numeral)

Report on Raid 13/9/16

Party left our trenches at 11.5 pm led by 2nd Lieut C.J. CARRUTHERS. They crawled to within 20x of enemy trench. This took some time as the moon was bright and they could see parties at work on the enemy wire. They were challenged when within 20x of German wire but subsequent events to point of their having been spotted before then. When they were challenged Mr Carruthers gave the order to charge and he with 4 or 5 others rushed the trench. Mr Carruthers and two or three men succeeded in crossing the parapet which was quite unprotected with wire at this point. They found that the rest of the party had not followed and after bombing the trench retired under a very heavy fire

104

2/ Carruthers got back but some of his men are believed to be missing.

That as 2nd Carruthers gave the order to charge a strong enemy party came out from his Right and advanced against the left flank of our party. Instead of following 2nd Carruthers the majority of his party engaged these men with bombs and are certain they inflicted casualties. Had they done as ordered down followed 2nd Carruthers there is little doubt that he would have been able to cut off this hostile party and made a considerable bag. As it was they engaged themselves in a bomb fight in the open in which the Officer in Rear seems to have been unable to control them whilst

108

Lt Carruthers was left quite
unsupported on the far side
of the enemy trench.
The Sergeant who was with
Lt Carruthers was badly wounded
and 3 of his own men who crossed
with him have not yet come in.
Lt Carruthers reports that

① There is a S. eastern of strong
point at K.29.b.2.8 is
nonexistent.
② The trench here is full of
water. He fell in on his way
back and went in up to his
neck.
③ Bombs were thrown from behind
the parados and also from pits
about 15ʸ in rear of the parados.
④ The enemy had strong parties
out all along on his wire. This
probably accounts for his opposing
line of flares.
⑤ What flares were fired came from
his second line.

(6) As soon as our party charged red rockets were fired and the enemy produced a bad barrage of shrapnel over our front line. (Red flares were also noticed in the raiding parties on right and left became engaged)

(7) Enemy used MGs from his second line.

Enemy fired several minenwerfer from SEREE up to LYLE COPSE, and opened a fairly heavy rifle and MG fire. Five rounds gun fire from a battery on each flank of the headed front, left they heaps doing after it had been fired three times.

In my opinion the raid probably inflicted considerable casualties on the enemy but failed in its true objective owing to the need

of the party just following
instructions, when they engaged
the party on their left instead
of following their officer.
I thank 2/Lieut CARRUTHERS.
C.H. did extremely well and
was unlucky not to have made
a success of the raid.

3.25 A.M.
14/7/16

J. Thicklee. Ult
1/W.Yorks Regt

Appendix C.

Orders & Reports on
attack of the night 20/21.
July 1916.

S E C R E T.

Ref. Trench Map
LA BOISELLE   144th INFANTRY BRIGADE ORDER NO. 77.
1/5,000.   -------------------------------------

1. An organised attack will be made by the Brigade to-night 20/21 July against points 20 - 62 - 90 and X.3.a.2.3.

2. Point 20 is allotted to 6th Gloucesters, the remaining points to 5th Worcesters.

3. 145th Inf: Bde., will attack simultaneously on our right against points 40 and 79.

4. Zero time will be communicated later but will not be before 2.30 a.m. 21/7/16.

5. The attack will be carried out after a short (2 minutes) intense barrage, the Infantry following up the barrage closely.

6. M.G. fire will be used to cover the attack and Stokes Mortars will cooperate under the orders of O.s'C attacking Bns.

7. All points gained are to be consolidated at once and communication opened to the rear as soon as possible.

                                              B Johnston
                                                    Captain.
                                              Brigade Major.
                                              144th Infantry Brigade.

Copies 1.2.3 - retained.
       4 - 48th Divn. (form information)
       5 to 10 Bde.Units.
       11 - 145th Inf: Bde.   do
       12 - 146th Inf: Bde.   do
       13 - 110th Bde. R.F.A.   do
       14 - Right Group R.F.A.   do
       15 - Signals.   do

SECRET.

144th INFANTRY BRIGADE.
AMENDMENTS & ADDITIONS TO ORDER NO. 77.

The following amendments and additions will be made to 144th Inf: Bde., Order No. 77 of to-day's date.

Para. (2)   Points 90 and 62 are allotted to 6th Gloucesters, 90 and X.3.a.2.3. to 7th Worcesters.

Para. (5)   For (3 minutes) - read (5 minutes).

New Para. (8)   4th Gloucesters will stand to at 2.30 a.m. and be ready to move up to reinforce if required, moving by points 93 - 98 - 13.

Copies 1.2.3 - retained.
      4 - 48th Divn.
      5 to 10 - Bde. Units.
      11 - 145th Inf. Bde.
      12 - 146th Inf. Bde.
      13 - 110th Bde. R.F.A.
      14 - Right Group R.F.A.
      15 - Signals.

Captain.
Brigade Major.
144th Infantry Brigade.

1/6th Bn. Gloucestershire Regiment.
-----------oOo-----------

Supplement to War Diary, July, 1916.

The following attacks will be made tonight 21st July, 1916.

"A" Company will advance its bombing post to between 2.c.3.8. and 2.c.3.9.

"C" Company will attack and consolidate 2.c.8.8., push a permanent bombing post towards 2.a.8.0. and bomb towards 2.d.2.8. to meet "D" Company

"B" Company supported by "D" Company will attack the line 2.b.2.0. (inclusive) to 2.b.6.2. (inclusive); simultaneously a Company of the 7th Worcesters will attack 2.b.6.2. (exclusive) to 2.d.9.0. (inclusive). This line 2.b.2.0. to 2.b.9.0. is to be consolidated and bombing posts established up all trenches leading to the front. "B" Company will deploy in 4 platoon waves just North of 2.d.2.6.

"D" Company will be in support in the trench - 2.c.7.1. - 2.c.9.2. - 2.d.0.2. They will be under the orders of O.C. "B" Company to assist in consolidating, or to replace casualties if O.C. "B" Company considers that he is not strong enough to hold the captured line.

O.C. "D" Company will detail 1 Lewis Gun and two bombing sections to follow in rear of "B" Company to make good 2.d.2.8. and to bomb from there towards 2.c.8.8. to meet "C" Company.

"C" & "D" Companies will be responsible for consolidating and holding the trench 2.c.8.8. - 2.d.2.8.

Central dump for bombs, S.A.A. and water will be formed at 2.d.0.2. under 2/Lieut. RUGMAN

O.C. "D" Company will be responsible for keeping O.C. "B" Company supplied when the objective has been captured.

Battalion Hdqrs. will move to 2.a.8.5., Hdqrs. of the 7th Worcesters.

"A" & "C" Companies will be connected by wire with Battalion Hdqrs. A wire will follow "B" Company and a station will be established where O.C. "B" Company may direct. Should telephone communication break down, runners will be employed

                                                (Sgd) J.Micklem,
                                                      Lt.Col.

1/6th Bn. Gloucestershire Regiment.

Supplement to War Diary, July, 1916.

Report on attack on the morning 21st July, 1916

Attacks were carried out in accordance with orders issued.

The attack by "A" Company on barricade at point 39 succeeded and by 3 am was in our hands. Shortly afterwards, however, the enemy began bombing down the trench and making use of small bombs to cover their approach, they succeeded in bombing our party defending the barricade, and in rushing it.

A further party was sent up to the attack and the barricade was again taken, but 10 minutes later the enemy rushed barricade and re-captured it. The party then retired to our old barricade at point 37 and the enemy did not attempt to rush this.

Casualties in this attack :-
    4 Killed
    25 Wounded

The attack was successfully supported by the Stokes Gun until ammunition failed.

The attack on point 88 succeeded and by 3-45 am "C" & "D" Companies were in touch on the line point 88 - point 29.

At about 4 am, enemy made an attempt to re-take point 88, making a bombing attack across the top. This, however, was successfully dealt with and driven off by our bombers and rifle and Lewis Gun fire.

Heavy casualties were known to be inflicted upon the enemy.

Casualties in this attack :-
    2 Killed
    25 Wounded

"B" Company, supported by "D" Company formed up for the attack on point 29 - point 62 from the trench running from point 26 towards point 47 and during the two minutes bombardment, worked their way forward.

When the barrage lifted they advanced to the attack but immediately came under very heavy machine gun fire from both flanks.

The two leading platoons suffered very heavy casualties and were unable to get near enemy trench. Capt. ELLIOTT commanding "B" Company was killed and 2/Lieuts. A.R. SMITH & H.E.H. SUTTON, severely wounded.

"D" Company of the 7th Worcesters on our right were also unable to get on and retirement came necessary.

Casualties in this attack :-
    3 Killed
    9 Missing
    33 Wounded

Appendix D.

Orders & Reports on
attack on night of 22/23rd
July 1916.

SECRET.

Ref. Map 144th INFANTRY BRIGADE ORDER NO. 79.
LA BOISELLE
1/5,000.

1. The attack will be continued tonight 22/23rd July, 1916.

   145th Bde., will attack on our right.

2. 8th Gloucesters forming up from point 47 due E. to the Railway, and advancing at zero, will capture the German trench from point 90 to point 40. Point 40 will also be attacked by 145th Bde.

   Points 20, 62 and 90 will be bombarded with Stokes Mortars from - 5' to + 5'.

   4th Gloucesters will hold the 1st and second lines and be prepared to hand over to 5th Royal Warwicks if required to reinforce the attack.

   7th Worcesters will be in a position of readiness about RIBBLE ST., at 2 a.m. 23rd July, with a view to reinforcing or continuing the attack.

   5th Royal Warwicks will send two companies to OVILLERS by 8 p.m. to-night. These Coys., will reconnoitre the 1st and 2nd lines and be ready to take over from 4th Gloucesters.

   2 Coys., 5th Royal Warwicks will be at CRUCIFIX CORNER at 8 p.m. and remain there in reserve.

   Brigade Machine Gun Company will cooperate according to instructions issued separately.

   A Brigade Adv. Report Centre will be established at X.8.c.09. to which place all reports will be sent.

   Zero time has been communicated to those concerned.

                                            Major.
                                       Brigade Major.
                                    144th Infantry Brigade.

Copies 1.2.3 - retained.
     4 to 9 - Bde. Units.
    10 - 5th R.War. R.
    11 - 48th Divn. (for information)
    12 - 145th Bde.   do
    13 - 143th Bde.   do
    14 - 144th Bde. R.F.A. } Left Group R.F.A.
    15 - Right Group R.F.A. }
    16 - 3rd Fd. Coy. R.E.
    17 - Signals.

C o ½ A. 90. Rt.
½ A. 90.
D. 3 Platoon Rt Rg
1   "   90.

B. B. H.Q.

a. 47 at 12
Tape due E sit 477
One T 150° from Rg
Another T. 225° from H.Q.
Covering party of tape RE party
entrench O. Relief 10.15. pm.

Dig trench from 78 to joining up of 450°
Distance to two big dugouts. 230.
1 Sec RE to new HQ.
Remainder of RE 11.30 pm new HQ.

1/6th Bn. Gloucestershire Regiment.
———————oOo———————

Supplement to War Diary, July, 1916.

ALL COMPANIES.

The following attacks will be made tonight 22nd July, 1916.

"C" and half "A" Company will attack point 94 and to the right of point 94.

Half "A" Company will attack point 90. Three platoons of "D" Company will support attack on right objective and one platoon on left objective.

"B" Company will be in Reserve at Battalion Hdqrs.

The assaulting columns will form up in platoon waves at 20 yards interval. A tape will be put out by R.E. on a line due East from point 47. There will be two "T's" off this tape -- one 150 yards distance from the Trench Railway, another 225 yards from the Trench Railway. "A" & "C" Companies will each find a covering party for tape R.E. party. They will be at the entrance to OVILLERS at 10-15 pm.

The right assaulting column will form up each wave successively on the tape line between the Railway and the 150 yards "T". The left assaulting column between the 150 yards "T" and the 225 yards "T".

One section of R.E. will be held in Reserve at Battalion Hdqrs. One section of R.E. will follow the last wave of the assaulting column.

ARTILLERY SUPPORT.

The enemy line will be bombarded for ten minutes at 8-30 pm tonight and intermittent fire will be maintained from 8-50 pm onwards.

"Zero" time for the attack:- 12-30 am.

Point 40 will be marked by Artillery always firing 4 rounds at a time. At point 90 two rounds at a time will be fired.

AEROPLANE CONTACT.

Seventy five flares will be carried by each Company and Contact Aeroplane will fly over the lines at 5 am, 8 am, 12 noon, 4 pm & 8 pm.

BATTALION HDQRS.

Battalion Hdqrs. during the attack will be at dug-out near point 78.

In the event of the attack failing, a second attack will be made at 4 am., Should it be found impossible to capture the enemy trench.

All ground gained will be maintained and men will dig in as far forward as possible. Equipment will be carried by different waves in accordance with instructions issued to O.C. Companies.

(Sgd) J. Micklem,
Lt. Col.

H.Q. 144th Inf Bde

Report on attack 12·30 a.m. 23rd July

Party of RE under Lt BRIGGS with a covering party moved off ahead of the Battn to place a tape on a due East line from pt. 47 to railway. Lt BRIGGS worked rapidly and well and the tape was fixed just before the head of the Battn reached the railway end of the tape.
The Battn moved through OVILLERS along the road and emerged at 78. They proceeded in single file along the left of the Railway and formed up on the tape behind the covering party. The area over which they had to move was being steadily shelled with 5.9″ but the men behaved well and the coys moved into their assaulting formation without a hitch.
At about 12.15 AM they started moving forward and though the shelling continued there were few casualties. Shortly

before zero the two leading waves were roughly 70° from their objectives and still moving steadily. At this point M.G. fire was opened from the front and from about 39 and 40 on the right. The fire was very accurate and the leading waves were cut down. The subsequent waves moved on but very few got through the zone of the M.G.s. As far as I can gather from statements of the few N.C.O.s and men who returned a party of about 6 men entered the enemy trench just N.W. of pt 40 and engaged the enemy with bombs. One of this party has returned. He states that he was captured and his equipment and bomb bag taken from him. However in the excitement he managed to get a bomb out of his pocket, this bomb he threw among his guard and in the confusion escaped. All the officers but one who started are casualties and information

is difficult to obtain but it
seems that the last waves
of the consolidating company
did not get into the zone of
M G fire. They state that they
saw the signals of the want
on their right while and retired
after them.
The following numbers have
reported unwounded up to the
present.

A Coy (left assault) 42.
C " (right) 29
D " (consolidating coy) 7.

Casualties were difficult to
collect as Gas shells were
fired on road 78 — 39 and
Sibbe helmets had to be worn,
but at 6.15 AM bearers and
stretchers were working in the
open quite unmolested up to
a line about East and West
through 47.
One of C Coys Lewis guns with
3 of its team is reported to
be lying in about 40th West
F 40.
Casualties among officers were

very heavy C & D Coys losing all their officers and only one coming in from A Coy. So far as I can gather they are as follow.

3 killed
2 probably killed
4 wounded and brought in
1 suffering from gas

The RE officer whose section went forward is also missing.

The cause of the failure was in my opinion the lack of artillery preparation. None of the MGs previously reported had been knocked out and the enemy had hardly been shelled at all. The barrage which I understood was to keep the enemy's heads down while the assaulting troops advanced was quite useless as there were long intervals when not a single shell burst on the front of the attack. The result of this was that the enemy MGs, having nothing to worry them,

were able to fire on the
assaulting troops as they
pleased.
From all accounts the men
behaved very well and pushed
steadily through a heavy
shell fire but the zone of
MG fire seems to have been
quite impassable.
The commanders of both leading
coys were killed and the
men who have returned state
that their behaviour was
magnificent. Particularly
W. PARAMORE. O.C. A Coy 4/5
they say behaved in the
war on the barrack square
though he was hit and taken
a very heavy fire from M.G.
Even after being hit in the
stomach he continued to
lead his men till he fell dead.
Reliable information is difficult
to obtain as all the officers
and nearly all the NCO's
of the leading coys are
casualties.

23/7/18

S. Mackler Lt
4/6 Rfjnhlkt

HQ 14th Bde

Information collected from men who
came in night 23rd/24th July after
attack 22nd/23rd July.

The men all state that the attacking
party started off all right in to
proper waves. When they approached
the German parapet they found good
wire and were held up by very
heavy M G fire. 2/Lt CORBETT and most
of the leading wave were killed. The 2nd
and 3rd waves came up under 2/Lt
BRACESTONE? who was killed. Major
COATES commanding the assaulting
troops then came up and was killed
as was 2/Lt DILLON who came up with
the next wave. Three other
Officers just behind were wounded and
thus accounted for all the officers. The
result of these waves coming up
was an irregular line of about
40 men with one Lewis gun dug in
about 20x from the German parapet.
They were under a very heavy fire
from MGs and were unable to send
back information about their situation.
They had been ordered before starting

to hang on to every foot of ground gained and to dig in and wait for a rearrangement attack if they failed to penetrate the German line. Acting on this order they worked joining up and improving shell holes till daylight when they found that the least movement drew heavy fire. They were shelled and sniped all day and withdrew with some casualties at dark July 23rd. A L/Cpl in charge of a Lewis Gun who was dug in about 40x West of Pt.40 (this is where he thinks he was) states that the wire was strong all along this part of the German line. He states that a M.G. was in action directly to his front and just to the right of that an English Lewis Gun. That to the right of him was an unoccupied German listening post which seemed to be connected to the German line by a mine gallery. He states he saw a large number of Germans who offered good targets but as all his ammunition drums but 4 had been buried he decided to keep his ammunition for defense in case he was rushed. He made them observation in daylight and he can probably be relied on.

There seems little doubt that on the left a small party got into the German trenches. Four men have come back who all tell roughly the same story. It seems that a party of 7 or 8 men got into the trench and engaged the enemy, they threw bombs and used their bayonets. After a time five of them were captured and disarmed but the enemy neglected to search their pockets for bombs. A large party of the enemy collected round them and seemed in a very excited state. A shell burst near and in the confusion two of them got bombs from their pockets, threw them and scattered the enemy. Four of the party (one wounded) then escaped and joined the remainder of their coy who were in shell holes on the edge of the German wire. They all state that the enemy trench was strongly held, and that they accounted for several of the enemy.

T. Nicklin, 2/Lt.
o/c 1/9th Yorks Regt

24/7/16.

144th Brigade.
48th Division.

1/6th BATTALION

GLOUCESTERSHIRE REGIMENT

AUGUST 1 9 1 6

Report on Operations 20th to 23rd August

WAR DIARY or INTELLIGENCE SUMMARY

(Erase heading not required.)

Army Form C. 2118.

AUGUST, 1916.   1/6th Glouc. Regt.

Hour, Date, Place		Summary of Events and Information	Remarks and references to Appendices
AUG 1st	FRANSU	In billets.	
AUG 4th	"	Battn reinoculated.	
4.30 pm AUG 8th	"	Regimental Sports	
6.45 am AUG 9th	"	Left billets.	
10.30 am	CANDAS	In billets.	
5.55 am AUG 10th	"	Left CANDAS and marched to PUCHEVILLERS. Bad Road. Wet.	
11.0 am	PUCHEVILLERS	In billets.	
7.0 am AUG 12th	"	Left Billets.	
12. noon	BOUZINCOURT	In billets.	
2.0 pm	"	Left billets and went into bivouac in field in V.12.a (Sheet 57.D.SE)	
12.30 pm AUG 13th	"	Left bivouac for trenches.	
5.0 pm	Trenches	N of OVILLERS. Took over line. 37.66.67.77.88.28.2b.47.90. (OVILLERS Trench map 1.5.000) from 7th E. SURREYS. During the night patrols sent towards pts 74 & 79. Enemy attacked & recaptured SKYLINE trench on our right during night.	
10.0 pm AUG 14th	"	B Coy attacked pt 62 unsuccessfully. 2nd Lt BARRINGTON wounded. B Coy attacked again at about midnight and A Coy attacked twice more before dawn. No attack made any progress owing to bright moonlight.	
3.0 pm AUG 15th	"	Relieved by 4th Glouc in the trenches. Went into Reserve trenches at RIBBLE St (E of AVELUY)	
3.0 pm AUG 16th	"	Were relieved by 5th R.WARWICKS. Went into billets at BOUZINCOURT.	

WAR DIARY
or
INTELLIGENCE SUMMARY.

(Erase heading not required.)

Army Form C. 2118.

AUGUST 1916.   1/6th Glouc Regt.

Hour, Date, Place	Summary of Events and Information	Remarks and references to Appendices
12.30 p.m. Aug 19th BOUZINCOURT	Left Billets.	
3.0 pm "	USNA Redoubt. In reserve shelters.	
4.30 pm Aug 20th TRENCHES.	Not OVILLERS. Relieved 5th R.WAR. on line 16-25-46-56-65-76 (excl)	A
	Operations of 20th. 21st, 22nd & 23rd described in Appendix A.	
10.0 am Aug 23rd "	On our left 4/5 Glouc. on our right 7th Worc.	
12 noon Aug 23rd BOUZINCOURT.	Were relieved in trenches by BUCKS Batt. In billets.	
2.50 pm Aug 26th "	Left billets.	
4.0 pm " FORCEVILLE.	In huts. 2 off 2nd Lts COWPER & DODSON (8th HANTS joined)	
5.15 pm " Trenches E. of AUCHONVILLERS.	Took over line Q10.c.2.1 - Q10.d.5.2 (BEAUMONT French map) from 9th SUFFOLKS.	
Aug 27th "	3 Officers. LIEUT. R.H. BALL. LIEUT. HARRISON (8th Hants) and 2nd LT COOMBS (8th Hants) joined.	
	The weather during August was mostly fine.	
	Bad spell between 28th - 30th.	
	Casualties during August. Killed Capt J.K. GILMORE. Aug.22nd.	
	2nd Lt WOODFORD Aug. 21st	
	missing. 2nd Lt CLARKE " 22nd.	
	Wounded. 2nd LT E. BARRINGTON. Aug. 14th.	
	Capt. J.V. BLAD. " 21st.	
	2nd LT HAWKINS. Aug. 21st.	
	Other Ranks. 20 killed. 20 wounded & 105 wounded.	
	The Strength of Batt'n is now 16 off and 292 OR below strength.	

1/6th Bn. GLOUCESTERSHIRE REGT.

ACCOUNT OF OPERATIONS FROM 20th to 23rd AUGUST 1916.

The Battalion took over from the 1/5th Royal Warwicks about 4 pm. 20th, "A" Coy. holding Front Line which ran 16, 18, 25, 46, 56.

By 8 pm. Capt. HARTOG had moved on the line to 19, 29, 27 and had barricades 50 yards N.W. of 19 and 70 yards S.W. of 31.

On the 21st about 5-30 am. the Germans made a weak attack against Barricade near 31 which was easily repelled. Between then and 12 noon we made three attempts to occupy 31. We occupied 31 for a short time but were bombed out. At 12 noon "B" Coy. had orders to take the line 31-51. Orders for this attack were received very late and the Coy. Commander only had 50 minutes to get his men in position. They consequently started late and failed to reach their objective.

About 6 pm. "C" Coy. took over front line from "A" Coy. "D" Coy. moved up in support and "A" and "B" were withdrawn.

Night of 21st/22nd was quiet. At 5 am. under cover of a thick mist the Germans attacked and collected under the bank immediately N. of 31-19 and broke in E. and W. of 19. The platoon holding trench N.E. of 19 was cut off and scattered. The platoon N.W. of 19 retired on the 4th Gloucesters via 81. The remainder of the Coy. was forced back on to the line 16-25-46, with small party holding on to the barricade 100 yards S. of 19.

O.C. "D" Coy. (Major NOTT) pushed out bombing parties, one in the direction of 19 and one in the direction of 27 via 25 and 46.

Two Machine Guns were mounted on the parapet between 16 and 19 where they covered the left front. While these guns were being mounted, No. 2019 Pte. KERR spotted a German Machine Gun coming into action in the open just N. of 19. He got up and knelt on the parapet where he was exposed in full view of the enemy and succeeded in shooting three members of the enemy machine gun team and prevented the gun opening fire. A Lewis Gun of the Royal Sussex Regt. who at the time of attack were just leaving our front line where they had been working, was mounted on 46. Capt. GILMORE commanding "C" Coy. was killed whilst organising a counter attack against 29.

Situation at 6-15 am. Enemy were holding 19-29-27. We were holding barricades 16 and 19, 16 and 27, 46 and 27.

Lieut. CLARE SMITH was in charge on the left and Lieut. FULLERTON on the right. A constant supply of bombs was organised and about 8 am. Point 27 was re-occupied. Enemy holding barricades at 29 and 19 and making large use of our bomb stores which they had captured there, still held out and after a time began to outthrow us. O.C. "D" Coy. then sent up a few selected bombers who altered the situation and we moved up one barricade nearer to 29. No. 2635 Acting Corporal GUNSTON particularly distinguished himself in this bombing from 27.

About 10-30 am. Lieut. COSTIN moved a Stokes Gun into trench between 25 and 46 and 2nd Lieut. HARRIS went up to our barricade S. of 19 and registered the line 19-31. O.C. "D" Coy. moved up two fresh platoons into readiness. The Stokes guns opened intense barrage on the line 19-31 at 11 am. They fired intense again at 11-30 and under cover of this, two platoons of "D" Coy. attacked. The right platoon found enemy all knocked out and re-occupied barricade N.W. of 29. Enemy at 19 had remained in his position, but the position was captured by the left platoon, all the enemy (11) being killed with the bayonet. This platoon got touch with the right platoon E. of 19 and re-occupied the barricade half way to 81.

About 1 pm. the remains of "C" Coy. were withdrawn and "D" Coy. took over all the front line. A patrol was sent out to 81 where six men of "C" Coy. were found and touch was gained with the

1/6th Bn. GLOUCESTERSHIRE REGT.

ACCOUNT OF OPERATIONS FROM 20th to 23rd AUGUST 1916.

The Battalion took over from the 1/5th Royal Warwicks about 4 pm. 20th, "A" Coy. holding Front Line which ran 16, 16, 25, 46, 56.

By 8 pm. Capt. HARTOG had moved on the line to 19, 29, 27 and had barricades 50 yards N.W. of 19 and 70 yards S.W. of 31.

On the 21st about 5-30 am. the Germans made a weak attack against Barricade near 31 which was easily repelled. Between then and 12 noon we made three attempts to occupy 31. We occupied 31 for a short time but were bombed out. At 12 noon "B" Coy. had orders to take the line 31-51. Orders for this attack were received very late and the Coy. Commander only had 50 minutes to get his men in position. They consequently started late and failed to reach their objective.

About 6 pm. "C" Coy. took over front line from "A" Coy. "D" Coy. moved up in support and "A" and "B" were withdrawn.

Night of 21st/22nd was quiet. At 5 am. under cover of a thick mist the Germans attacked and collected under the bank immediately N. of 31-19 and broke in E. and W. of 19. The platoon holding trench N.E. of 19 was cut off and scattered. The platoon N.W. of 19 retired on the 4th Gloucesters via 81. The remainder of the Coy. was forced back on to the line 16-25-46, with small party holding on to the barricade 100 yards S. of 19.

O.C. "D" Coy. (Major NOTT) pushed out bombing parties, one in the direction of 19 and one in the direction of 27 via 25 and 46.

Two Machine Guns were mounted on the parapet between 16 and 19 where they covered the left front. While these guns were being mounted, No. 2019 Pte. KERR spotted a German Machine Gun coming into action in the open just N. of 19. He got up and knelt on the parapet where he was exposed in full view of the enemy and succeeded in shooting three members of the enemy machine gun team and prevented the gun opening fire. A Lewis Gun of the Royal Sussex Regt. who at the time of attack were just leaving our front line where they had been working, was mounted on 46. Capt. GILMORE commanding "C" Coy. was killed whilst organising a counter attack against 29.

Situation at 6-15 am. Enemy were holding 19-29-27. We were holding barricades 16 and 19, 16 and 27, 46 and 27.

Lieut. CLARE SMITH was in charge on the left and Lieut. FULLERTON on the right. A constant supply of bombs was organised and about 8 am. Point 27 was re-occupied. Enemy holding barricades at 29 and 19 and making large use of our bomb stores which they had captured there, still held out and after a time began to outthrow us. O.C. "D" Coy. then sent up a few selected bombers who altered the situation and we moved up one barricade nearer to 29. No. 2635 Acting Corporal GUNSTON particularly distinguished himself in this bombing from 27.

About 10-30 am. Lieut. COSTIN moved a Stokes Gun into trench between 25 and 46 and 2nd Lieut. HARRIS went up to our barricade S. of 19 and registered the line 19-31. O.C. "D" Coy. moved up two fresh platoons into readiness. The Stokes guns opened intense barrage on the line 19-31 at 11 am. They fired intense again at 11-30 and under cover of this, two platoons of "D" Coy. attacked. The right platoon found enemy all knocked out and re-occupied barricade N.W. of 29. Enemy at 19 had remained in his position, but the position was captured by the left platoon, all the enemy (11) being killed with the bayonet. This platoon got touch with the right platoon E. of 19 and re-occupied the barricade half way to 81.

About 1 pm. the remains of "C" Coy. were withdrawn and "D" Coy. took over all the front line. A patrol was sent out to 81 where six men of "C" Coy. were found and touch was gained with the

4th Gloucesters. This patrol also brought in some of our wounded men who had been captured but subsequently left behind by the enemy. Patrol was also sent out along trench 27-79. This trench was found to be unoccupied except by an enemy sentry 50 yards W. of 79.

At 5 pm. "A" Coy. took over the front line and "D" Coy. remained in support. About 7 pm. another patrol went through towards 79 and got touch with 7th Worcesters just S. of that point.

About 8-30 pm. enemy attacked barricade N.W. of 29 using a large quantity of high explosive and smoke bombs. He almost captured the barricade, wounding the whole of the garrison with the exception of Lieut. TITLEY.

Lieut. TITLEY and 2897 Sgt. PEARCE (who had been knocked out by a bomb but had recovered) just managed to hang on. Two platoons of "D" Coy. were moved up into close support but did not become engaged. Stokes Mortars opened a heavy fire on 31 and from 31 down to our barricade.

About 10-30 pm. enemy shelled our front line heavily and buried one stokes gun and 200 rounds of ammunition. During the night the enemy made three more attacks on this barricade but in each case were easily driven off. At 2 am. Lieut. POOLE took out a patrol and reconnoitred ground N.W. of trench 19-31. He found all trenches within 100 yards N. of 19 had been abandoned by the enemy and "A" Coy. moved up to old barricade 70 yards S.W. of 31 without opposition. A very large number of enemy dead were found in and about the trench between 19 and this barricade.

After daylight the enemy made no further attacks and this line i.e. from 70 yards S.W. of 31 to 81 exclusive was handed over to Bucks Battn. about 11 am.

24/8/16

J. Micklem
Lieut. Col.
Comdg. 1/6th Gloucester Regiment.

144th Brigade.

48th Division.

1/6th BATTALION

GLOUCESTERSHIRE REGIMENT

SEPTEMBER 1 9 1 6

WAR DIARY
or
INTELLIGENCE SUMMARY

SEPT. 1916
1/6th GLOUC. Regt

Army Form C.-2118.

(Erase heading not required.)

Instructions regarding War Diaries and Intelligence Summaries are contained in F.S. Regs., Part II. and the Staff Manual respectively. Title pages will be prepared in manuscript.

Hour, Date, Place	Summary of Events and Information	Remarks and references to Appendices
5.10 am Sept. 3rd THIEPVAL.	Attack by 39th and 49th Div. on our right. Were heavily shelled by heavy howitzers from 8.0 am – 3.0 pm.	During the 2 month of September weather was good except some bad spells on 18th and 29th.
3.0 pm Sept. 6th AUCHONVILLERS	Were relieved by 16th KRR on left. and 9th SHERWOOD FORRESTERS on right. Went into billets at Bus. Motor buses from MAILLY.	Casualties
9.30 am Sept. 13th BUS	Were inspected on 9th by GOC 48th Div. Bus left billets.	Officers Nil. O.R. 7 killed. 8 wounded.
1.0 pm " " AMPLIER.	Arrived at huts. Found them uninhabitable marched to SARTON	Strength of Battalion is now 1 officer over strength and 90 OR under strength.
6.0 pm " " SARTON.	In billets.	
7.30 pm Sept 18th SARTON.	Left billets marched to BOISBERGES. Very wet.	
2.30 pm " " BOISBERGES.	In billets.	
" 21st – 23rd	Battalion Rifle meeting.	
" 24th	Bde Rifle meeting. We secured the first three prizes.	
" 28th	Div Attack scheme on BERNAVILLE	
8.50 am " 30th	Left for SUS-ST-LEGER.	
3.30 pm " 30th	Arrived in billets.	

J. Micklem Lt Col
Comdg 1/6th Glouc Regt.
1/10/16

18B
1 map

144th Brigade.

48th Division.

1/6th BATTALION

GLOUCESTERSHIRE REGIMENT

OCTOBER 1 9 1 6

Army Form C. 2118.

WAR DIARY
or
INTELLIGENCE SUMMARY.
(Erase heading not required.)

OCTOBER 1914 1/6 Gloucester Regt.

144/48

Instructions regarding War Diaries and Intelligence Summaries are contained in F.S. Regs., Part II. and the Staff Manual respectively. Title pages will be prepared in manuscript.

Hour, Date, Place			Summary of Events and Information	Remarks and references to Appendices
10.30 am	1st	SUS-ST-LEGER & WEDGEON	Moved off.	Sunny October
1.30 pm	1st	HALLOY	In billets.	The weather was
11.0 am	3rd	HALLOY	Moved off. Cold march.	on the whole very
2.0 pm	3rd	ST AMAND	In billets.	wet
2.0 pm	4th	ST AMAND	Moved off blocked in GRENAS.	
6.0 pm	"	HALLOY	In billets.	
	5th	GRENAS	D. Company moved to the Chateau.	Casualties
	6th	SAILLY	Working party of 500 Emergency Cables.	2nd Lt KINNEAR wounded
9.45 am	10th	HALLOY	Left billets. Disappearing column at GRENAS.	on 18th and 2 N.C.O.
12 noon	10th	HUMBERCOURT	In billets.	
2.0 pm	13th	HUMBERCOURT	Left billets.	Strength of Batt'n
5.30 pm	13th	ST AMAND	In billets.	now 4 officers 600
5.30 pm	16th	Trenches Took over line from K.3.d.3.6 & K.3.c.0.1 (HEBUTERNE trench map) from E.R. Lancashires.		Strength 60 OR under Strength
5.40 pm	19th	Trenches	Relieved by 4th Kokls.	Strength
9.30 pm	19th	ST AMAND	In huts.	
9.0 am	20th	"	Moved off.	
1.45 pm	20th	SUS-ST-LEGER	In billets.	
	24th	TALMAS	Transport moved to TALMAS.	
9.10 am	25th	SUS-ST-LEGER	March off to IVERGNY. Entrained in French buses	
5.0 pm	25th	BRESLE	In billets. Transport arrived from TALMAS.	
9.0 am	31st	BRESLE	Marched off by platoons.	
12.30 pm	"	ALBERT	In billets.	

J. Nisbet
Lt Col Comg
1/6 Glouc Regt.
1/11/16

Vol 19
19R

144th Brigade.

48th Division.

1/6th BATTALION

GLOUCESTERSHIRE REGIMENT

NOVEMBER 1 9 1 6

CONFIDENTIAL

WAR DIARY Vol 20
of
1/6th GLOUCESTER REGT

From 1st to 30th Nov. 1916

(Vol. XX)

WAR DIARY
or
INTELLIGENCE SUMMARY.
(Erase heading not required.)

Army Form C. 2118.

NOVEMBER, 1916. 1/6th GLOUC. Regt

Hour, Date, Place	Summary of Events and Information	Remarks and references to Appendices
1.30 p.m. Nov.1st ALBERT	Moved by platoons to SCOTT'S Redoubt. X.21.b.34 (Albert Sheet)	Remarks
5.0 p.m. " SCOTT'S Redoubt.	All in.	
9.0 p.m. Nov.2nd Reserve Trenches.	Took over trenches from 9th Black Watch. Relief complete 9.0 p.m. HQ in M.27.d. CRESCENT ALLEY. (Geudecourt Trench map)	Weather. Generally dull & cloudy. Heavy rain from 24th - 26th.
Nov 3rd "	1 Coy in FLERS line M.22.a.81. 1 Coy in CRESCENT ALLEY. 2 Coys in PRUE Trench.	
	Bde g. moved to M.27. C.20. in MARTINPUICH. Working parties on trenches in LESARS. 5 OR. killed 2. wounded.	Strength of Batt. is now 1 officers over establishment. 190 OR. under strength
10.0 p.m Nov.5th LE SARS	Relieved 8th WORC. in line from M.10.C.20 – M.16.d.68. B Coy on left. D Coy on right. A in support in Sunken Rd. M.16.d. C Coy in reserve in FLERS Support line M.22.a. Enemy artillery active, wet. Casualties killed. 4. wounded. 11.	
10.30 p.m Nov 6th "	Little quieter. Casualties 2 nd Lieut SCORE wounded. OR. 3 killed	
" Nov 7th "	Relieved by. 1/4th Glouc. R. Quiet Relief. 1. 1 Killed 2. wounded.	
3.0 Am " Nov 8th SCOTT'S Redoubt.	All in. Very wet.	Casualties during month.
3.0 p.m Nov 8th – 20th "	Finding working parties.	
" "	Left Camp.	
9.15 p.m " EACOURT L'ABAYYE	Took over trenches in front of BUTTE DE WARLENCOURT. from 1/5th WORC. R. line from M.17.C.09 – M.17.d.0085 (Geudecourt map) A&C Coys in front. B in support. D in Reserve. HQ at M.22.d.70.	1 Officer wounded. OR. killed 16. wounded. 40.
11.15 p.m. Nov.23rd "	Fairly quiet trip. Foggy but fine. Relieved by 1/7th R. Warwick.	
2.30 Am " 24th BAZENTIN. WOOD.	In shelters	
Nov 28th VILLA Camp.	A B.C. and . HQ moved to Camp. E of CONTALMAISON.	

T. K. S. [?] Lt-Col
Comdg 1/6th Glouc Regt

144th Brigade.

48th Division.

1/6th BATTALION

GLOUCESTERSHIRE REGIMENT

DECEMBER 1 9 1 6

Vol 21

21.R
2 sheet

Confidential

War Diary
of.
1/6th Gloucestershire Regiment

From 1st December 1916 to 31st December 1916

Volume 21.

WAR DIARY
or
INTELLIGENCE SUMMARY

1/6th GLOUCESTER REGT. Army Form C. 2118.

(Erase heading not required.)

DECEMBER 1916.

Hour, Date, Place	Summary of Events and Information	Remarks and references to Appendices
8.0 pm. 1st Trenches	EUCOURT L'ABBAYE. Took over support trenches from 1/7th R. Warwicks. Lines held as before. Both 'A' & 'D' Coy at SEVEN ELMS. 'B' and 'C' Coys in PRUE TRENCH. 'A' Coy in STARFISH. Dull and frosty weather.	During December the weather was changeable throughout. 1st – 5th frosty. 5th – 14th Snowy & wet. 15th – 20th wet. 20th – 27th Fair. 28th – 31st Showery.
8.30 pm. 5th Support Trenches.	Relieved by 1/8th R. Warwicks.	
10.0 pm. SHELTER WOOD.S. Camp.	In huts.	Casualties
8th "	'E' (working) Coy of 2 off + 80 OR formed.	O.R. Killed 2
9.0 pm. 9th TRENCHES.	Took over trenches from 1/8th R. Warwicks. Lines held as on Nov 20th.	Died of wounds 1 Wounded 10
5.30 pm. 12th "	Relieved by 1/7th WORCESTERS moved back to support positions as on 1st.	
9.30 pm 14th "	Relieved by 10/11 H.L.I.	Strength of Battalion is now 50 officers over establishment. 260 O.R. under.
12.30 am. 15th SHELTER WOOD CAMP	Bad Camp & bad weather in tents.	
1.20 pm 16th MAMETZ WOOD.	Moved into camp at X.23.b.5.5.	
22nd "	" " Camp shelled.	
12.30 pm 25th FRICOURT Camp.	All in huts.	
2.30 pm 29th BECOURT Camp.	A. All in huts.	
2.30 pm 30th CONTAY.	In billets. Marched via ALBERT – BRESLE. Heavy wind.	

J Walkelett
Major
Comdg 1/6th Glouc Regt.

22.R
2 enest

Vol 22

Confidential
War Diary
Hart Bu reau centripetic type
from Tel out Star January 1917
(Volume XXII)

Army Form C. 2118.

WAR DIARY
or
INTELLIGENCE SUMMARY. 1/6th GLOUCESTER. REGT.

JANUARY.
1917.

(Erase heading not required.)

Instructions regarding War Diaries and Intelligence
Summaries are contained in F. S. Regs., Part II.
and the Staff Manual respectively. Title pages
will be prepared in manuscript.

Hour, Date, Place		Summary of Events and Information	Remarks and references to Appendices
2.45 pm. 6th	CONTAY	Inspected by LIEUT-GEN. W.P. PULTENEY. K.C.B., K.C.M.G., D.S.O Commanding III Corps.	The weather during January was cold and showery till the 8th from that date very severe frosts with some snowfalls were experienced.
7.0 am. 7th	"	Transport left village and marched to ST SAVEUR. marching on to HUPPY next day. Lt Col T. MICKLEM D.S.O posted as instructor at Senior Infantry officers School at ALDERSHOT. Major T.W. NOTT took over Command	
4.55 am. 8th	"	Paraded and marched to MEILLY	
9.0 am "	MEILLY	Entrained.	
12.30 pm "	PONT REMY	Detrained and marched to HUPPY. Bad march in blizzard	Casualties during month. Lieut F.D. RUGMAN and 1 O.R. accidentally wounded on 25th.
3.45 pm "	HUPPY.	In billets.	
	"	Training.	Strength of Battalion is now 8 Officers over strength and 245 O.R. under strength.
2.2	HALLENCOURT	Bde Attack Exercise	
2.3	"	"	
6.0 pm. 26th	HUPPY.	Transport left Battalion and marched to ARGOEUVES moving on to AUSIGNY on 27th and to CERISY on 28th.	
2.50 pm. 28th	"	Paraded and marched to OISEMENT	
6.0 am 28th	OISEMENT.	Entrained.	
1.15 pm "	WARFUSEE	Detrained and marched to CERISY.	
3.0 pm "	CERISY.	In billets.	

A.H. Bennett, Capt
Comdg 1/6th Glouc Regt.

Vol 23

23 R.
7met

Confidential

War Diary

of

1/6th Bn Gloucestershire Regt.

Feby 1st to 28th 1917

(VOL XXIII)

Army Form C. 2118.

WAR DIARY
or
INTELLIGENCE SUMMARY.
(Erase heading not required.)

February, 1917.   1/6th Gloucester Regt.

Instructions regarding War Diaries and Intelligence Summaries are contained in F.S. Regs., Part II. and the Staff Manual respectively. Title pages will be prepared in manuscript.

Hour, Date, Place	Summary of Events and Information	Remarks and references to Appendices
8.0 A.M. 1st. CERISY.	Left billets. marched via MORECOURT – MERICOURT – FROISSY – CAPPY – Camp 56. Arriving 12.noon. Could not get into camp till 4.30 p.m.	
3.30 p.m. 2nd Camp 56.	Left camp by platoons. marched VIA ECLUSIER – HERBECOURT Dressing Station	
5.0 p.m. 2nd HERBECOURT.	Pret by Guides. A Coy remained Camp 56 as working Coy.	
8.45 p.m. 2nd Trenches.	Relieved the 13th Batt. 135th Regt. FRENCH INF in trenches N of BARLEUX. 2 Coys in line One In support – N.12.b.45 – O.I.d.15. (BARLEUX Sheet Operations See Appendix. A. 1:10.000.)	Appendix. A.
8.45 A.M. 7th "	Relieved by 1/7th Worc. Regt.	
2.15 A.M. 8th MARLY.	Went back to D.V. Res. Huts. Mr. A+S Coy at MARLY. C+D Coy at FROISSY.	
12.noon. 10th MERIGNOLLES.	Station, A Coy sent to unload ammunition.	
9.0 p.m. 12th MARLY.	C+D Coys moved from FROISSY.	
4.0 p.m. 16th "	A Coy rejoined.	
2.0 p.m. 17th "	Left Camp for trenches by platoons.	
4.0 p.m. " G.28.b.45. (Shut 62.c)	Hours halt for Tea.	
12.20 A.M. 18th Trenches.	Relieved BUCKS Batt: Relief delayed on left. Line now extended to S. Held from N.12.Q.90.05. to O.I.d.15. 3 Coys in line 2nd LTs. DIBBLE wounded on patrol. Severe Thaw. Trenches 1 in support. became rapidly very bad.	During February the weather was very cold + frosty up till 11th. From 11th – 17th a period of slight thaw. followed by rain on the night of 17th/18th and a heavy Thaw. 18th to 28th Generally dull. Casualties during the month Are. 2nd Lts STEPHENS and DIBBLE wounded O.R. Killed. 15. Wounded. 21.
2.30 A.M. 22nd "	Were relieved by 1/7th Worc. Regt. Bad Relief owing to darkness and mud. All in Brigade Reserve. C Coy in FLAUCOURT.	
5.30 A.M. 24th RAVINE ACHILLE.	25 cases Trench Feet.	Strength of Battn is now Officers soon to establishment
7.0 p.m. 24th "	Relieved by 4th OXFORD + BUCKS. L.I.	3000 R. " "
11.0 p.m. 24th Camp 56.	All in. Working parties.	

Walker Lt Col
Comdg 1/6th Glouc Regt

1/3/17.

1/6th Bn Glouc. Regt.

Supplement to War Diary
February 1917.

Appendix "A"

1/6th Bn. Gloucestershire Regiment.

Supplement to War Diary February, 1917.

8-45 pm Feb. 2nd.	We relieved the 135th French Regiment in Sector "D", MAISONETTE Trenches.
3-30 am Feb. 3rd.	Situation normal, weather frosty. - quiet night.
3 pm " "	Situation normal. Enemy registered important points in our lines with trench mortars and field guns. Casualties:- 1 O.R. wounded.
6 - 6-30 am. Feb. 4th.	Enemy continued registration.
8am - 12 noon. "	Enemy carried out a systematic bombardment of our wire, front line trenches, subsidiary communication trenches, 2nd line, reserve line and main communication trenches. Bombardment carried out by trench mortars, field guns, 10 cm & 15 cm howitzers.
12 - 1 pm. " "	Short respite.
1 - 4-30 pm " "	Bombardment continued. 3-30 pm. Casualties:- 3 O.R. killed, 3 O.R. wounded. Wire and trenches in general, very badly damaged - PIGALE levelled in places. Trenches POMMIERS & MAUPOIL very badly blocked in several places.
5-30 pm. " "	Enemy opened drum fire barrage on our trenches, trench mortars and field guns firing on our front line.
5-50 pm. " "	Enemy attempted to raid our Right Company.

Reports on raid as under :-

Provisional Report on attempted German Raid on Sector "D" held by 1/6th Bn. Glouc. Rgt. on 4/2/17.

"At 5-30 pm after a bombardment which had lasted intermittently since 6-30 am, the enemy opened a barrage on our lines which lifted at 5-50 pm. Two parties of the enemy then rushed at our trenches between BOYAH NEGRO and CHEMINADE".

"Our men were standing to in their shelters along with the M.G. on the right of sector. Our men at once manned the trench and the M.G. opened fire on the enemy advance."

"A small number of the enemy penetrated our trench, several were killed between our wire and the parapet, the remainder fled. The left party did not reach our lines at all. Those who reached the trench were disposed of by bayonet and bomb. Three enemy were killed and one wounded in the trench. The operation was over by 6-15 pm. At 6-30 pm, on receipt of the first report along with the Intelligence Officer, I went to the Right Company Hdqrs. and then to the front line, and found all quiet. Several enemy were lying in front of our parapet and an examining patrol has gone out to obtain identifications".

"The enemy barrage interrupted communication in our main and subsidiary communication trenches, Support and Reserve trenches are stopped in a few places, and front line is badly knocked in".

"No attempt was made to raid our left subsector".

"Detailed reports as to casualties sustained by us and inflicted on the enemy, are not yet to hand from front Company Commanders".

"The wounded German is at present being sent down for examination."

"Our French Artillery Liason Officer gave us the artillery support we asked for. Further details will be forwarded as soon as received."

"All precautions had been taken in the event of an attack or raid. Detailed orders had been given to Company Commanders and were carried out. At 5-30 pm when the enemy barrage opened, we at once, through the liason officer, got our artillery to open a counter-barrage. We kept his lines under fire till the situation was quiet."

(Sgd) R.F.Gerrard, Capt.
Comdg. 1/6th Glouc. Regt.

Supplementary Report on attempted German Raid on Sector "D" held by 1/6th Bn. Glouc. Regt. on 4/2/17

"The enemy strength was about 100 and they appear to have come over in 2 waves. When the barrage lifted they at once came under the fire of our rifles, machine guns and lewis guns. As soon as they reached our trenches they were at once disposed of. The enemy were driven back leaving 9 killed and 1 wounded prisoner."

"A large number of unexploded German bombs have been found in and around our trench. Three of the enemy dead were carrying rifle grenades, and one a torch light, presumably for examining dug-outs. German rifles and three wire cutters were also found by our men".

"No identification marks were to be found on enemy dead. They were not wearing tunics, only waistcoats, and over them greatcoats, from which the shoulder straps had been removed. They had no documents in their possession. They were wearing steel helmets. None of the enemy dead had their bayonets fixed. Bayonets were carried in scabbards in the usual way. The enemy dead were all big men."

"During the operation, 3 Frenchmen who had been taken prisoner by the enemy, were found by our men. They were sent back to their Regiment via Battalion Hdqrs., with a guide."

"Our casualties during the afternoon amounted to 8 killed and 15 wounded, of whom 5 have returned to duty, and at present one of our men is unaccounted for. There is a great amount of heavy debris in the front trench and it is probable he may have been buried. Steps are being taken to clear this matter up".

"In addition to enemy casualties stated above, it is probable that our barrage will have cost him further losses in and around his own trenches.

Report on work of Machine Gun on Sector "D" (1/6th Glouc. Regt.) during raid.

"The only gun which was required to repel the attack was that placed on our right flank near the junction of BOYAU CHEMINADE with the front trench. This gun performed excellent service. As soon as the enemy barrage lifted, the team opened fire and accounted for several of the enemy and caused others to turn tail and go back to their own trenches. The behaviour of the crew was most creditable."

"As far as can be ascertained, none of the other guns on our sector had an opportunity of opening fire".

(Sgd) R.F.Gerrard, Capt.
Comdg. 1/6th Glouc. Regt.

The following Officers, N.C.O's and men were recommended for their work during the raid -

    Lieut. J.A.FLETCHER
    2/Lieut. G.STEPHENS.

    No.20402 Corpl. Padfield
    No.20282 Pte.   Quigley
    No. 3759 Pte.   Rose.

3-30 am Feb. 5th.	Situation quiet.

3-30 pm Feb. "	Situation normal. Casualties during the bombardment and raid on 4th:-
	    2/Lieut.G.Stephens; slightly wounded.
	    Other Ranks : Killed 8
	                     Wounded 15

3-30 am Feb. 6th.	Situation normal, weather frosty.
3-30 pm Feb. "	Enemy appeared to be checking their ranges on our lines and for a time it was thought he intended to attempt another raid. Precautions were taken but nothing occurred. Casualties:- 1 O.R. wounded.
February 7th.	Normal day, except enemy shelled MAUPOIL with 15 cm shells during the afternoon.
8-45 pm " "	Relieved by 1/7th Worcester Regiment.

---oOo---

Confidential

1/6th Bn. Gloucestershire Regiment

WAR DIARY FOR MARCH 1917.

VOLUME 24.

1/6th B. Gloucestershire Regt.

Supplement to War Diary

March 1917

Appendix A

1/6th Bn. Gloucestershire Regt.

Supplement to War Diary March, 1917.

REPORT ON FIGHTING PATROL

When patrol was ordered Support & Reserve Companies were in the middle of relieving the Front Line, and this was not complete till after 1 am. The ingoing Company on the right had not been in that sector before, and consequently there was some delay in collecting and organising the patrol; especially as it takes a runner ½ hour to get to Front Line from Company Headquarters and all movement over the top between midnight and 3 am was impeded by enemy machine gun fire sweeping this sector from some position on our right. An Officer patrol had gone out before the Fighting patrol was ordered and this patrol went out to N.12.b.8.3. and moved in an Easterly direction along the enemy wire. There was no sign of enemy posts here but very lights were going up both right & left. This patrol returned about 2 am.

The Fighting patrol under Lieut. BYARD (consisting of a platoon 20 strong) left our lines at about N.12.b.75. After proceeding South for 120 yards they ran up against two belts of thick wire. No gaps being found the patrol started cutting a gap at about N.12.b.65.25 and this was complete by 4-30 pm without opposition. The patrol then entered and moved to the right along DANIEL ALLEY and the Sap, and then back along DANIEL ALLEY to N.12.b.71. There was no sign of the enemy in their trenches. Some of the trench was filled with wire, there were several dug-outs which were entered by some of the patrol but found empty. There was a M.G.Emplacement at about N.12.b.70.15 with a dug-out close by, also empty. There were also several snipers plates in position on the right. A lot of new stick grenades were lying in front of the parapet. As it was then after 5 am and getting light, Lieut.BYARD returned with his platoon reaching our front line at 5-15 am. The only sign of the enemy was a sniper who fired from the enemy reserve line, about 5 rounds and what looked like 3 men were observed dimly at about N.12.b.30. just before the party left. Otherwise, no notice was taken of the patrol's operations, but very lights were going up from enemy's front line both to right and left from which Lieut.BYARD deduced that there were a few small posts holding the line, but DANIEL ALLEY is apparently not held at all.

Meanwhile, a patrol of 1 Officer & 2 O.R. from the Left Company left our lines at O.1.c.3.1. and reached the wire at O.7.a.9.9. Here they were fired on by a post which also put up a very light. The patrol then returned.

I have issued orders for a stronger Officers patrol to take advantage of the mist, if it lasts, and try and get in the enemy trench at this point. The getting through of orders, messages and information, and the drawing of bombs etc. was a very slow process especially owing to the relief and the tired condition of the runners, and this explains the delay in starting off the patrols.

(Sgd) T.Walker Nott,
Lt.Col.
15/3/17. Comdg. 1/6th Bn. Glouc. Regiment.

Confidential

Vol 25

War Diary
of
1/6th Bn. The Gloucestershire Regt. (T.F.)

From 1/4/17 to 30/4/17

(Vol. XXIV)

25.12
22 sheets

WAR DIARY
or
INTELLIGENCE SUMMARY.
(Erase heading not required.)

Army Form C. 2118.

Instructions regarding War Diaries and Intelligence Summaries are contained in F.S. Regs., Part II. and the Staff Manual respectively. Title pages will be prepared in manuscript.

Hour, Date, Place	Summary of Events and Information	Remarks and references to Appendices
A.O.H. 1st March 1915	At Camp 5b. Working Parties	
2nd	— do —	
3rd	March 3 Coys. & R.E. Sects. to dig & consolidate trenches in support positions	
	Headquarters at 27.36 a.04. Relief complete 10.5 p.m.	
4th	to trenches	
5th	— do —	
6th	— do —	
7th	Relieved by 1 Coy. 5th Glouc. & 1 Coy. 4th Royal Berks. Relief complete 9 p.m.	
8th	to Camp 5b	
9th	do. Working Parties	
10th	do	
11th	do	
12th	All Camp Clean. Relieved 5th Glouc. in Right Front Trenches.	
13th	Relief complete 11:00 p.m.	
	In trenches.	
14th	— do —	
15th	Information received from Brigade at 9 p.m. and reports that some of our troops were advancing, that the enemy	
	were withdrawing in our front and that our 4th Corps attack in Neuve Chapelle direction was pushing forward.	
16th	Asked to send out patrols	
17th	Patrols out.	
	G.O.C. Division ordered an attack on a strong pt. This took place at 3.30 pm. It appears our bombardment commenced lightly. Scale was made, and it told on Coys. and in conjunction with German Ry Landau on our left and Flanders, the enemy front opening was overwhelmed by more severe, all counting to & very heating falling. Was relieved by reserves at 11 pm.	
18th	Moved back to SOPHIE tunnel	
19th	All to SOPHIE	
20th	SOPHIE tunnel	

Army Form C. 2118.

WAR DIARY
or
INTELLIGENCE SUMMARY.
(Erase heading not required.)

Instructions regarding War Diaries and Intelligence Summaries are contained in F. S. Regs., Part II. and the Staff Manual respectively. Title pages will be prepared in manuscript.

Hour, Date, Place	Summary of Events and Information	Remarks and references to Appendices
Mar 21st	Moved to Camp K. all in Tents	
22nd	" Camp K	
23rd		
24th	Received orders to move to PERONNE 10.30 am. Head of Column arrived PERONNE 7 pm.	
25th		
26th	In Billets PERONNE	
27th		
28th		
29th	Left PERONNE 2.30 pm. Took over outpost line from 5th & 6th Chasseurs	
30th	Covered in an attack on ST EMILIE, which was captured. Holding outpost line.	
31st		
	Casualties 5 O.R. Killed 13 O.R. wounded 2 Officers 368 Other Ranks } Sick.	
	Weather during month Stormy.	

[signature]
Lieut. Col.
Comdg 2/4 East Lancs Regt.

Forms/C. 2118/10.

WAR DIARY
INTELLIGENCE SUMMARY

(Erase heading not required.)

Army Form C. 2118.

1/6 Bn Gloucestershire Regt.

Hour, Date, Place	Summary of Events and Information	Remarks and references to Appendices
EPEHY April 1st	Batt. attacked EPEHY at 5.0 AM - see Appendix A - relieved by 7th Worcester Regt. at 9.0 PM - on relief Batt. moved back to VILLERS FAUCON and became Bde Reserve.	JMC
VILLARS FAUCON " 2nd 5 3 2	Sinking parties found -	JMC
" 3rd	Reinforcement of 9 OR received.	JMC
" 3rd	- Batt. Bde Reserve at MARQUAIX.	JMC
MARQUAIX 4th - 7th	Batt. stood to in reserve to Bde attack on LEMPIRE & RONSSOY	JMC
" 7th	Batt relieved 1/5 Gloucester Regt at Camp near St EMILIE	JMC
ST EMILIE 8th	Moved to camp behind railway embankment at E.29.b.55.	JMC
OUT POST LINE 9th	Took over outpost line from 7 Worcesters at 11.30 PM from F.8.6.85	JMC
" 11th	to F.10.c.33	
" 11th	Relieved in outpost line by the 1/6 Gloucester Regt: - 1 OR wounded	JMC
	and 1 limber wagon smashed by shell fire - moved back to	
Camp at E.29.6.55	Camp at E.29.6.55.	
" 12th	"C" Coy took over outpost line from 4 Gloucesters Regt.	JMC
" 13th	Remainder of Batt. Moved to RUITOYRE WOOD at 6.0 AM to relieve at 7.0 AM	JMC
	"B" Coy was moved forward to RONSSOY WOOD stopping 1/2 Gloucesters	
	Regt. and relieved to camp about 12 noon.	JMC
	Batt relieved at 6 Camp by 1st Bucks Batt: & to outpost	JMC
MARQUAIX 16th - 16th	line by 5 Gloucester Regt. - on relief Batt moved to MARQUAIX	JMC
" 16th	Working parties found.	JMC
	Batt. moved to VILLARS FAUCON	JMC
VILLERS FAUCON 17th	Batt. moved to at 4.0 AM ready to support 145 Inf Bde attacking	JMC
	GUILLEMONT FARM	

Army Form C. 2118.

WAR DIARY
or
INTELLIGENCE SUMMARY.

(Erase heading not required.)

1/6th Bn. Gloucestershire Regt.

Instructions regarding War Diaries and Intelligence Summaries are contained in F.S. Regs., Part II. and the Staff Manual respectively. Title pages will be prepared in manuscript.

Hour, Date, Place	Summary of Events and Information	Remarks and references to Appendices
VILLERS FAUCON April 17th	The following reinforcement received :- 2nd Lieut H. C. DARRACOTT & 46 O.R.	JMC.
" 18th	The letter enclosing in Battn HQ Officers was blown up at 5:55AM. The explosion was due to a German mine with a delayed fuze. The following officers were killed thereby:- Lieut-Col T. M. NOTT D.S.O. - Major R. F. GERARD - Capt & adjt L.E. NOTT M.C. Capt L. E. HARRISON R.A.M.C. (attached 1/6 Glouces Regt) - Capt M. F. BURGESS Lieut L. KING M.C.	JMC.
" 19th	Capt J. H. CROSSKEY 1/5 R. War. R. was allotted to the Battn; & took over the command. - Capt B. A. LAIRD R.A.M.C. joined Battn as M.O.	JMC.
Out-post line 20th	Battn took over the out-post line from 1/5 Gloucester Regt	JMC.
" 21st	HQ + 2 out-post line in TEMPLEUX FARM. Reinforcement of 42 O.R.	Ref Burness orders Appendix B. JMC.
St EMILIE 22nd-23rd	Battn relieved by the Gloucester Regt - arriving neo to St EMILIE	JMC. Ref Officer's orders Appendix C.
Out post line 23rd	Battn relieved the Gloucester Regt to outpost line about 9.15PM at 3.45AM attacked the ground known as the KNOLL. -	Ref Officer's Orders Appendix D. JMC Ref Appendix E.
" 24th	Battn's dale cursing outpost line, as the dispositions were readjusted - 1 Coy holding outpost line from TEMPLEUX FARM - 1 - LEMPIRE - Coy holding post for out "BROWN" Line	JMC.
" 25th	Battn relieved L- at St EMILIE by 1st Bucks Battn - after relief Battn moved to broken by 1/5 Gloucester Regt & to Tincourt Reinforcement of 21 OR received:-	JMC.
TINCOURT 26th - 28th	Battn finding working parties. Major H. St G. SCHOMBERG - East Surrey Regt joined Battn; took over command.	JMC.
" 27th		JMC.

Major H. St G. SCHOMBERG - East Surrey Regt. joined Battn; took over command.

Army Form C. 2118.

1/6th Bn. Gloucestershire Regt.

WAR DIARY
or
INTELLIGENCE SUMMARY.
(Erase heading not required.)

Instructions regarding War Diaries and Intelligence Summaries are contained in F.S. Regs., Part II. and the Staff Manual respectively. Title pages will be prepared in manuscript.

Hour, Date, Place	Summary of Events and Information	Remarks and references to Appendices
TINCOURT April 28th	Battn. moved to VILLARS FAUCON taking over Bivouacs & Billets of 1/4th Gloucesti. Regt.	JdC
VILLARS FAUCON 29th	Battn. moved up to the out-post line & relieved 1/5th Glouc. Regt - 24 O.R. No 1 Regt. (Int. OR. Div. No. 1)	JdC
OUTPOST LINE. 30th	Battn: Holding outpost line in front 3 to 4 Cos. Right of TOMBOIS FARM. - 129th Bde Ist Aust. Div. 5th Regt. and 6th Regt. on the right. - Reinforcement of 13 OR received.	JdC JdC

Patrol Return Night 30.4.17.
Officers 27.
O.R. 569.

Total Casualties

Officers { 8 killed
          { 5 wounds.

O.R. { 3 killed
      { 82 wounded
      { 12 missing.

A.J. Schomberg
Major
Comdg 1/6th Gloucestershire Regt.

1/6th Bn. Glouc. Regt.

Supplement to War Diary - April 1917.

Appendix A

1/6th Bn. Gloucestershire Regiment.

Battalion Operation Order. — March 31st 1917.

1.   The Battalion will attack EPEHY tomorrow in conjunction with the WARWICK Brigade on the left and the 7th Worcesters on the right. Forming up point from North corner of CAPRON COPSE - E.17.d.9.9. Right flank of the Battalion during advance, VILLERS FAUCON - EPEHY Road. Left flank on a line from the North end of CAPRON COPSE to station in F.1.a. Touch must be kept with the 7th Worcesters on the right, and the Warwicks on the left.

2.   The Battalion will form up as per enclosed sketch - "A" Coy. on the Right, "C" Coy. on the Left, "D" Coy. in Reserve. with the exception of the platoon of "C" Coy. now on Advanced Post which will join in in its correct place as the Battalion advances. The Battalion must be in position by 4-30 am.
    O.C. "A" Coy. must be prepared to assist "C" Coy. in taking up correct position. O.C. "D" Coy. will move his Company off along the road past Battalion Hdqrs. and report to Battalion Hdqrs. by 3 am. "C" Coy. should start not later than 3-30 am. "A" Coy. not later than 4 am. Zero is 5 am. at which time all four Battalions will advance in Artillery formation as per sketch, until the light makes it necessary to shake out into formation shown in sketch No.2.
    Battalion Hdqrs. will move at head of "D" Coy.
    "B" Coy. will relieve the "D" Coy. platoon now on Advance Post, with a platoon, and will remain in those positions unless the Warwicks go through them.

3. DUMPS.   Packs and Mess stores for "D" Company to be dumped at quarry E.15.a.8.7. - of "A" & "C" Coys. at or about their present Hdqrs. 1 senior N.C.O., 1 Lewis Gunner, Mess steward & 2 batmen per Company will remain with these packs. One Officer with experience per Company will also be left behind

4. DRESS & EQUIPMENT.
    Dress: Fighting order, iron rations, filled water bottles and tomorrow's rations. Tools will be carried by the two rear platoons of the front Companies and 50% of each platoon of "D" Coy. in the proportion of, as far as possible, 2 shovels to 1 pick. Very pistols, very lights flares and wire-cutters must be taken.

5.   Regimental Aid Post will be at "C" Coy. present Hdqrs.

6.   Contact Aeroplane will come over EPEHY at 7 am or later. On its arrival, flares will be lit by all Coys.

7. ARTILLERY SUPPORT.
    The advance will be made in the dusk without Artillery support, unless the S.O.S. is sent up by O.C. Battalion, when Artillery would fire for 5 minutes into EPEHY. This procedure would hold good each time S.O.S. went up.
    At 6-30 am barrage will be placed along line of the Railway in F.1.b. Slow rate of fire will be maintained for 20 minutes. When Battalion succeeds in entering the village "C" Coy. will be responsible for clearing the street from E.6.d.9.7. to F.1.a.5.6. and "A" Coy. from F.1.c.3.5. to F.1.a.7.4.

8.   The Eastern edge of the village will be consolidated as soon as possible and barricades erected to block the streets.

9.   A visual signalling station will move with "A" & "C" Companies.

10.   WARNING.   No men except stretcher bearers must come back with casualties until operations are over; then only by orders of O.C. Company. Men slightly wounded should endeavour to carry on.

If prisoners are taken, only small escorts should be sent with them to Battalion Hdqrs. Once the advance has started, all should press on at a steady pace. Bunching must at all cost be avoided.

It is absolutely essential that Companies are in their places punctually.

31/3/17.

(Sgd) T.W.NOTT,
Lt.Col.
Comdg. 1/6th Bn. Glouc. Regiment.

1/6th Bn. Gloucestershire Regiment.

Report on attack on EPEHY, 1st April, 1917.

(Ref. Operation Order "A" att.)

The Battalion less "B" Coy. formed up in position and moved forward at 5 am. The Artillery formation was preserved until the leading platoons were about 150 yards short of the village, then, on the enemy opening a brisk rifle fire from the outskirts of the village, the platoons extended and pressed forward. No serious obstacles were encountered and, as it was then getting light a belt of very weak wire in which were numerous gaps, failed to hamper the attack.

The village was entered at about 5-50 am, the enemy making no serious resistance until the objective, the railway bank East of the village was reached. Here rapid fire was exchanged and in places where the enemy was close enough, he used bombs. As it was close on 6-30 am, "A" & "C" Coys. had to retire from the railway bank as our guns were to place a barrage along the bank at 6-30 am. As soon as the barrage ceased, "A" & "C" Coys. moved forward again and consolidated the position along the railway bank

The enemy commenced to shell the Western side of the village; later he shortened his range and fired into the village, and finally at about 6-50 am he attempted to barrage the railway bank. He showed no signs of counter attacking and confined his attentions to shelling, the railway bank with field guns & 4.2's, and the village mostly with 4.2's, 5.9's & 8".

As soon as the consolidation was nearly completed, "A" & "C" Companies thinned out the front line, withdrawing troops to the cellars at the Eastern extremity of the village. "D" Company were established in cellars at the Western end of EPEHY - VILLERS FAUCON Road, about 200 yards short of the village.

Casualties during the attack -

Killed: 1 Other Rank.

Wounded: 9 Other Ranks.

29/4/17.

Lieut. & A/Adjt.

1/1th Bn. Glouc. Regt.

Supplement to War Diary – April 1917.

Appendix "B"

1/6th Bn. Gloucestershire Regiment.

Battalion Operation Order   -   April 19th 1917.

Ref.Map 62C N.E. 1/20,000 Ed. 3a.

1.   The 144 Infantry Brigade will relieve the 145 Infantry Brigade today, the 6th Gloucesters relieving the 5th Gloucesters in the Left Battalion Sector.

2.   The Battalion will move off in the order -

Hdqrs. "A" "B" "C" "D"
by platoons at 100 yards interval. 100 yards interval will also be kept between Hdqrs. and the leading platoon of "A" Company. Battalion Hdqrs. will pass the level crossing in E.23.d.2.1. at 7-45 pm. Route: ST.EMILIE - Road junction F.21.c.3.9. there will be guides from the 5th Gloucesters -

    1 guide for Battalion Hdqrs.
    1   "   " each Coy. Hdqrs.
    1   "   "   Platoon.

Dress: Fighting Order, men will wear greatcoats and box respirators in the alert position.

3.   The dispositions of the Battalion will be as under -

    "A" Coy. on the Right will relieve "A" Coy. 5th Glouc.
    "B" Coy. "   " Left   "   "   "B" Coy. "   "
    "C" Coy. in Reserve   "   "   "C" Coy. "   "
    "D" Coy. "   "   "   "   "D" Coy. "   "

4.   Lewis Gun limbers and Officers' Mess limbers will proceed with the Battalion and will be unloaded at road junction F.21.c.3.9. "A" & "B" Coys. Lewis Gun limber in rear of the leading platoon of "A" Company, "C" & "D" Coys. Lewis Gun limber in rear of the leading platoon of "C" Coy.
        Officers' Mess limbers for "A" & "B" Coys. in rear of last platoon of "A" Coy., "C" & "D" Coys. limber in rear of last platoon of "C" Company.
        All other transport - tool wagons, S.A.A. the cookers of "A" & "B" Companies and Medical cart will proceed by the route: ST.EMILIE - Road junction F.19.b.4.9. - Road junction F.14.b.2.2. and will dump tools etc. at Battalion Hdqrs. at F.15.a.9.4. The cookers will remain in positions now occupied by those of 5th Gloucesters, "C" & "D" Coys. cookers will move to the Transport Lines.

5.   All S.O.S.Signals and wire-cutters will be taken up by Companies.

6.   Battalion Hdqrs. and Report Centre will be at LEMPIRE (F.15.a.9.4.). Relief complete will be reported as soon as possible.

19/4/17.

Lieut. & A/Adjt.

N O T I C E.

1.   O.C. Companies will see that all their billets in VILLERS are left clean and in good order.

2.   All men must proceed to the trenches with their water bottles full.

3.   One Officer per Company will be left behind and will stay at the Transport Lines under the command of Capt.J.A.Fletcher.

------oOo------

1/6th Bn. Glouc. Regt.

Supplement to War Diary - April 1917.

Appendix C

1/6th Bn. Gloucestershire Regiment.

Battalion Operation Order   April 21st. 1917.

===

1.   The Northern boundary of the 144th Inf. Bde. will run as follows -
Railway from level crossing at E.23.d.5.1. - F.8.c.93. - May Copse, (inclusive to this Brigade) - a point 200 yds. N.W. of TOMBOIS FM. - Canal at A.3.08. - VENDHUILLE exclusive to the Brigade - THE KNOLL (Low Hill at A.1.d.90.) is inclusive to the Brigade.

2.   The Inter-Battalion boundary will run as follows -
S. corner of RONSSOY WOOD (F.21.a.1.2.) - F.17.c.0.0. - MACQUINCOURT FM. (inclusive to Left Battalion).

3.   In accordance with paras 1 & 2 above, "B" Coy. 6th Glouc. Regt. will hand over tonight to 4th East Lancs. Battn. their two posts, one at F.4.d.9.9. and one at about point F.5.c.72. and "A" Coy. 6th Glouc. Regt. will take over from 8th Worcesters their left post at about point F.17.b.80.

4.   The platoon of the 4th East Lancs. Regt. relieving "B" Company will be at the cross roads F.4.b.19. at 8-45 pm. O.C. "B" Coy. will arrange for guides to meet them there to guide them to their positions.
        O.C. "A" Coy. will arrange details of relief of left post 1/8th Worcs. direct with the O.C. their left Coy.

5.   In continuation of the above, O.C. "B" Coy. will arrange to relieve O.C. "A" Coy. in his post at about point F.11.b.4.5. on the left of the TOMBOIS FARM - VENDHUILLE Rd. All the above reliefs will take place as soon after dusk as possible

6.   After these adjustments, the inter-Company line will be cross roads F.11.b.13. - F.6.d.00.- TOMBOIS FM. being inclusive to Left Company.

7.   The Battalion will be relieved tonight by the 1/4th Gloucester Regt. who will take over the new dispositions.

8.   "A" Coy. 4th Glouc. will relieve "A" Coy. 6th Glouc.
        "D" Coy. 4th Glouc.   "   "   "B" Coy.   "   "
        "C" Coy. 4th Glouc.   "   "   "D" Coy.   "   "
        "B" Coy. 4th Glouc.   "   "   "C" Coy.   "   "

9.   Guides 1 per Company, H.Q. and 1 per platoon will be at crater by the entrance to RONSSOY F.21.c.39. at 8-45 pm.
O.C. "D" Coy. will send an Officer to superintend and see that incoming Coys. get their correct guides.

10.   After relief, platoons will move independently to camp now occupied by the 4th Gloucesters at ST.EMILIE, by the following route:- Road junction F.21.c.39. - Road junction F.19.b.49. - ST.EMILIE.

11.   Transport for Lewis Guns, Mess Stores, etc. will be at cross roads F.15.d.88. by 8-30 pm.

12.   All Company Stores including S.O.S. Signals will be brought out. O.C. Coys. who have petrol cans for water in their possession will arrange to send them back to water carts by Battalion Headquarters before 9 pm.

13.   Separate orders have been issued to T.O. and Q.M.

                                        Lieut. & A/Adjt.
21/4/17.

1/6th Bn Glouc Regt.

Supplement to War Diary - April 1917.

Appendix "D"

SECRET. COPY NO. 5.

144th INFANTRY BRIGADE ORDER NO. 173

Ref. Maps 1/20,000
62 C. NE. & 62 B. SW.

23/4/17.

1. In co-operation with Brigades on either flank, the Brigade will attack and capture the enemy positions from GILLEMONT SPUR (A.1.3.) - KNOLL (A.1 & 7).

2. The attack will be carried out by 8th Worcesters on the Right, and 6th Gloucesters on the Left. Dividing line between Battalions from road junction F.11.d.9.8. to MACQUINCOURT FM (A.3.d.)
Objectives.
   Right Battalion. Where road crosses 140 contour in F.24.a. thence forward across spur East of GILLEMONT FM. to 120 contour about A.7.d.12 O.C. 8th Worcesters will also detail a party to attack and capture copse and high ground in A.19.d.
   Left Battalion. From 129 contour about F.12.c.9.7. - KNOLL - Cross roads in F.6.c.
Assemble positions.
   Right Battalion. Road in F.17.b. & F.11.d.
   Left Battalion   Road in F.11.b. & F.5.d.
   These will be protected by small posts thrown forward but not so far as to disturb the enemy. If the roads are unsuitable the R.E. will lay out tapes.

3. Both Battalions will push home the attack on their Left flanks, i.e they will come on to their objectives from a North-Westerly direction.

4. Zero hour will be 3-45 am. 24th April. Before that hour all assaulting troops will be in their assemble positions and all move forward at zero hour.

5. A copy of Artillery Programme is issued to O.C. 8th Worcesters and 6th Gloucesters.
   Up to 4-15 am. S.O.S. will bring 5 minutes barrage on the objective after that hour a 5 minutes barrage 300 yards East of objectives.
   At 4-15 am a protective barrage will be put on all approaches whether S.O.S. be sent up or not.
   Only one Officer with each Battalion is to have the signal, and it will not be taken by Right flank party attacking COPSE in A.19.d.

6. O.C. 144th M.G.Coy. will push forward 1 section in readiness to take up positions as soon as the attack as succeeded. Guns will be placed on both flanks of the KNOLL and on both flanks of GILLEMONT SPUR.

7. After capture of the objectives, troops will be thinned out as the situation permits. In consolidation, neither GILLEMONT FM. nor the actual summit of the KNOLL will be occupied. These points however will be denied to the enemy, and the valleys in between and on the flank must be protected by cross fire.

8. In preparation for the above, 8th Worcesters and 6th Gloucesters will relieve 7th Worcesters and 4th Gloucesters in the line tonight.
   7th Worcesters however will leave 2 Coys. and 4th Gloucesters 1 Coy in their support positions at the disposal of O.C. 8th Worcesters and 6th Gloucesters respectively.
   The 7th Worcesters less 2 Coys. on relief, will move to Camp at F.25.a.8.6.

9. O.C. Platoon Cyclists will maintain touch between the Brigade and the Brigade on our left by means of a patrol on MALASISSE FARM - LEMPIRE ROAD. He will also detail two orderlies to report to O's.C. 6th Gloucesters and 8th Worcesters by 10 pm today.

(Sgd) C.J.MITCHELL, Major,
Brigade Major,
144th Infantry Brigade.

SECRET.   COPY NO. 5.

144TH INFANTRY BRIGADE ORDER NO. 173

Ref. Maps 1/20,000
62 C. NE. & 62 B. SW.

23/4/17.

1. In co-operation with Brigades on either flank, the Brigade will attack and capture the enemy positions from GUILLEMONT SPUR (A.1.3.) - KNOLL (A.1 & 7).

2. The attack will be carried out by 8th Worcesters on the Right, and 6th Gloucester on the Left. Dividing line between Battalions from road junction F.11.d.9.2. to MAGQUINCOURT FM. (A.3.c.).
    Objectives.
    Right Battalion. Where road crosses 140 contour in F.24.a. thence forward across spur East of GUILLEMONT FM. to 130 contour about A.7.d.12
    O.C. 8th Worcesters will also detail a party to attack and capture copse and high ground in A.18.d.
    Left Battalion. From 130 contour about F.12.c.9.7. - KNOLL -
    Cross roads in F.6.c.
    Assemble positions.
    Right Battalion. Road in F.17.b. & F.11.d.
    Left Battalion.   Road in F.11.b. & F.5.d.
    These will be protected by small posts thrown forward but not so far as to disturb the enemy. If the roads are unsuitable the R.E. will lay out tapes.

3. Both Battalions will push home the attack on their Left flanks, i.e they will come on to their objectives from a North-Westerly direction.

4. Zero hour will be 3-45 am. 24th April. Before that hour all assaulting troops will be in their assemble positions and all move forward at zero hour.

5. A copy of Artillery Programme is issued to O.C. 8th Worcesters and 6th Gloucesters.
    Up to 4-15 am. S.O.S. will bring 5 minutes barrage on the objective after that hour a 5 minutes barrage 300 yards East of objectives.
    At 4-15 am a protective barrage will be put on all approaches whether S.O.S. be sent up or not.
    Only one Officer with each Battalion is to have the signal, and it will not be taken by Right flank party attacking COPSE in A.19.d.

6. O.C. 144th M.G.Coy. will push forward 1 section in readiness to take up positions as soon as the attack as succeeded. Guns will be placed on both flanks of the KNOLL and on both flanks of GUILLEMONT SPUR.

7. After capture of the objectives, troops will be thinned out as the situation permits. In consolidation, neither GUILLEMONT FM. nor the actual summit of the KNOLL will be occupied. These points however will be denied to the enemy, and the valleys in between and on the flank must be protected by cross fire.

8. In preparation for the above, 8th Worcesters and 6th Gloucesters will relieve 7th Worcesters and 4th Gloucesters in the line tonight. 7th Worcesters however will leave 2 Coys. and 4th Gloucesters 1 Coy in their support positions at the disposal of O.C. 8th Worcesters and 6th Gloucesters respectively.
    The 7th Worcesters less 2 Coys. on relief, will move to Camp at F.26.a.8.8.

9. O.C. Platoon Cyclists will maintain touch between the Brigade and the Brigade on our left by means of a patrol on MALASISSE FARM - LEMPIRE ROAD. He will also detail two orderlies to report to O,'s.C. 6th Gloucesters and 8th Worcesters by 10 pm today.

(Sgd) G.J.MITCHELL, Major,
                     Brigade Major,
                     144th Infantry Brigade.

1/6th Bn. Gloucestershire Regiment.

Battalion Operation Order   -   23rd April, 1917.

1. On the early morning of the 24th instant, the 144 Infantry Brigade will attack and capture the German position from the KNOLL in F.6 and 12 and A.1 and 7 to GILLEMONT FARM and SPUR in A.13 both inclusive.

2. The Brigades on either flank will be carrying out operations at the same time.

3. The 6th Gloucesters will attack on the left, the 8th Worcesters on the right. Dividing line for Battalions MACQUINCOURT FARM in A.3.c.

4. The objective for Left Battalion will be from cross roads in F.6.c. - KNOLL - to 120 contour about F.12.c.9.7.

5. "A" & "B" Companies 6th Gloucesters will carry out the attack -
    "B" Coy. on the Left.
    "A" Coy. on the Right.
These Companies will form up prior to the attack along the road in F.5.d. and F.11.b.
The right of "A" Company will be about 250 yards N.E. of the road junction F.11.b.0.3.
"C" Company will be in Support and will form up with two platoons in the sunken road in F.11.b. and two platoons behind the bank along the road between point F.11.c.8.6. and F.11.a.9.0.
"D" Company will take over as soon after dark as possible the present outpost line held by the 4th Gloucesters, and will hold this line.
1 Company, 4th Gloucesters will be attached to the Battalion and will be in Reserve in cellars at the East end LEMPIRE.

6. Companies will pass the fallen gasometer on the RONSSOY Road at the following times -
    "D" Coy. 8-15 pm.
    "A" Coy. 10 pm.
    "B" Coy. 10-40 pm.
    "C" Coy. 11 pm.
and will proceed by platoons at 100 yards interval.
Route: Road junction in F.19.b. - Road junction at F.21.c.4.9. - RONSSOY - LEMPIRE - TOMBOIS FARM. Dress: Fighting Order, wearing greatcoats. Box Respirators to be in the alert position. Iron rations and rations for the day must be taken - water bottles must be full.

7. Zero will be 3-45 am before which hour all assaulting troops will be in their assemble position.

8. Up to 4-15 am the S.O.S. will bring 5 minutes barrage on the objective, after that hour, the barrage will be 300 yards in front of objectives. At 4-15 am a protective barrage will be put on all approaches whether the S.O.S. has been put up or not. O.C. "B" Company will have charge of this signal.

9. O.C. 144 M.G.Coy. will have two guns in readiness to take up positions on both flanks of the KNOLL.

10.	After the position has been captured, the troops should be thinned as far as the situation allows. In consolidation the actual summit of the KNOLL should not be occupied, but this point must be denied the enemy, and the valleys in between and on the flanks must be protected by cross fire.

11.	Separate orders have been issued to the Transport Officer.

W. H. Coombs
Lieut. & A/Adjt.

9 am.
23/4/17.

Copies to :-

    1 & 2   War Diary.
    3 - 6   Companies.
      7   144 Infantry Brigade.
      8   Q.M. & T.O.

---------oOo---------

ADDENDUM.

Battalion Hdqrs. and Report Centre will be established by 2-45 am at point F.16.a.9.8. Advanced Report Centre will be in a dug-out in the sunken road at point 11 b.3.2.

Aid post will be in LEMPIRE by Battalion Hdqrs. The M.O. will arrange to have notice boards placed showing the way there.

Advanced dump of tools, S.A.A. and Bombs will be formed prior to the attack near TOMBOIS FARM (about point F.11.b.1.3.

Pack ponies with S.A.A. and tools will be stationed at East end of LEMPIRE.

---------oOo---------

1/6th Bn Glouc. Regt.

Supplement to War Diary - April 1917.

Appendix E

1/6th Bn. Gloucestershire Regt.

Operations carried out against the "KNOLL"
on April 24th 1917.
-----oOo-----

On the morning of April 24th, the Battalion attacked, in conjunction with the 1/8th Worcestershire Regt on the right and the 126th Infantry Brigade on the left, the high ground in F.6.C, F.12.A, A.1.D. & A.7.B. known as the Knoll -- Ref. Bde. Operation Orders attached. *1/6 Glouc: Operation orders (appendix D)*

"A" & "B" Companies, the assaulting Companies, formed up in two lines on the road in F.5.d. and F.11.b., "A" Coy. on the right, "B" Coy. on the left, with the right of "A" Coy. just N.E. of TOMBOIS FARM.

"C" Company formed up in support with
   (1) 2 platoons on the road between the points
      F.11.b.1.3. & F.11.c.9.8.
   (2) *2 platoons in the sunken road between pts F11.G.13 & F11.G.60*

"D" Company were detailed to hold the original outpost line. The Company of the 1/4th Gloucesters, which was attached to this Battalion was kept in Reserve at the East end of LEMPIRE.

At 3-45 am, "A" & "B" Companies advanced against the KNOLL with 2 platoons each in support.

After the Companies advanced about 200 yards, the enemy opened a heavy rifle and machine gun barrage.

The 1st attacking line reached the objective but the 2nd line lost objective and got broken up, failing thereby to support the 1st line. Owing to this the attacking force was outnumbered by the enemy and after considerable hand to hand fighting, both Companies returned to their original assemble positions, where they reformed. O.C. "C" Company was then ordered to throw forward 2 fighting patrols from the right of TOMBOIS FARM. Both of these patrols came under heavy rifle fire as soon as they showed themselves over the skyline and retired again to their original disposition.

Orders were then received from the 144th Infantry Bde. to suspend operations for the day.

The attacking Companies thereupon were ordered to retire to LEMPIRE, "D" Company remaining in the original outpost line with "C" Company in support.

Casualties during the attack :-

   Killed: Second Lieut.J.F.BROWN (16th Glouc. att.)
              Second Lieut.A.PEARS.
              2 Other ranks.

   Wounded: Lieut.R.H.BALL
              Second Lieut.J.G.SHUTTLETON(5th H.L.I. att.)
              Second Lieut.W.H.S.ROSE
Wounded. (At duty) Second Lieut.A.R.COOMBS (8th Hants. att.)
              Second Lieut.A.H.WATTS
   Wounded: 72 Other ranks.

   Missing: 12 Other ranks.

Died of wounds: 2 Other ranks.

                                   Major,
Comdg. 1/6th Bn. Gloucestershire Regt.

1/6th Bn. Glouc. Regt.

Supplement to War Diary - April 1917.

Operation Orders.

1/6th Bn. Gloucestershire Regiment.

Battalion Operation Order No.1.   April 29th 1917.

Ref. Map 62C. N.E. Edition 3a. 1/20,000.

1. **RELIEF.** The Battalion will relieve the 5th Gloucesters in the Left Front Sector tonight.

2. **DISPOSITIONS.** The dispositions of the Battalion will be -
   "A" Coy. on the Right.
   "B" Coy. on the Left.
   "C" Coy. Right Support
   "D" Coy. Left Support.

3. **MOVE.** The Battalion will move by platoons at 150 yards interval, in the order :-
   Hdqrs. "A" "B" "C" "D"
   Leading platoon of "A" Coy. to pass the level crossing, E.23.d.2.1. at 8-15 pm. Dress: Fighting order, men will wear greatcoats, and box respirators at the alert position.

4. **ROUTE.** ST.EMILIE - RONSSOY - LEMPIRE.

5. **GUIDES.** Guides will meet the Battalion at the crater at the entrance to RONSSOY at 9 pm.

6. **STORES.** Officers' valises will be dumped at the old Battalion Headquarters, VILLERS FAUCON at 2-30 pm.
   1 limber for Lewis Guns will be at the old Battalion Headquarters, VILLERS FAUCON at 7-45 pm, and will follow the leading platoon of "A" Coy. Guns will be drawn from the limber at cross roads LEMPIRE F.15.d.65.85.
   "A" & "C" Coys. surplus Lewis Guns will go back to the Q.M.Stores by the returning ration limbers.
   1 limber for Hdqrs., 1 for "A" & "B" Coys. & 1 for "C" & "D" Coys. stores for trenches will be at the old Battalion Headquarters VILLERS FAUCON at 7-45 pm. These limbers will be unloaded at the cross roads LEMPIRE F.15.d.65.85
   1 limber for mess stores not intended for trenches will be at the old Battalion Headquarters VILLERS FAUCON at 8 pm.
   The water carts will accompany the Battalion and will be left at the usual stand at about F.15.a.7.7.
   Coy. chargers will report to Coy. Hdqrs. at 8-15 pm., Hdqrs. at 8-45 pm.

7. **COMPLETION OF RELIEF.**
   Completion of relief will be reported to Battalion Headquarters by the code word "STONE".

29/4/17.

Lieut. & A/Adjt.

Reference Battalion Operation Order No.1.   29/4/17.

The following alterations will be made :-

Para 2.   "A" Coy. will be on the Right.
             "B" Coy. will be in the Centre.
             "D" Coy. will be on the Left.
             "C" Coy. will be in support in LEMPIRE.

Each Company in the line will find 2 platoons in the front line and 2 platoons in support.

Para 3.   Order of march will now be -

             "A"   "B"   "D"   "C"   Hdqrs.

Time as before.

                                        A.F. Coombs
29/4/17.   Lieut. & A/Adjt.

NOTICE.

As little movement as possible is to take place by day.

All Companies will take up all S.O.S. Signals and gas alarm signals, e.g. rockets.

----oOo----

No 26

Confidential

14/48

War Diary
of
No the Enveticeshire Regt

1er May to 31er May 1914

(VOL. XXVI)

26.R.
12mat

Army Form C. 2118.

WAR DIARY
or
INTELLIGENCE SUMMARY.
(Erase heading not required.)

1/6 Bn. Gloucestershire Regt.

Hour, Date, Place		Summary of Events and Information	Remarks and references to Appendices
OUTPOST LINE	May 1st	Batt. holding outpost line in a taken over from 75 Gloucester Regt.	
" "	May 2nd	Batt. relieved in outpost line by 6th Bn. Lancashire Fusiliers after relief moved to VILLARS FAUCON	Ref. O.O. No. 2 [sig]
VILLARS FAUCON	May 3rd	Batt. in billets at VILLARS—	
" "	" 4th	Batt. moved to Gap. 6 G. BUIRE (S26 d 88. Ref. map 62c) 2nd Lt. C.A. Smith, 2nd Lt. J. Southgate and 2nd Lt. R.J.T. Matheson joined	Ref. O.O. No. 3 [sig]
BUIRE	" 5th	for duty at BUIRE Training at BUIRE	
	" 6th	do.	
	" 7th	do. 143 other Ranks joined for duty	
		Capt. J.H. Gayshay rejoined 143 2nd Pdrs. Majo. W. Adams, 17th. Bn. Manchester Regt. posted to the Batt. as 2.i.c. in Command &	
		Instructor in duty. Lt. D.F. Harris rejoined Batt. for duty.	
	" 8th	Training. 2nd Lt. F.D. Rayburn rejoined the Batt. 9 other Ranks joined	
	" 9th	do. "	
PERONNE	" 10th	do. Lt. F.W. Brosnan posted to Batt. & appointed Acting Adjutant.	
	" 11th	Batt. moved to Villers [?] PERONNE. Billeting.	
COMBLES	" 12th	Batt. moved to COMBLES. Coy Commanders Lt. Gen Sir W. Pulteney	Ref. O.O. No. 4.
	" 13th	addressed the Brigade and presented decorations.	Ref. O.O. No. 5
FREMICOURT	" 14th	Batt. moved to FREMICOURT all in 4 hrs.	
	" 15th	Training. Lt-Col. A.W.G. Schomberg evacuated to F.A.	Ref. O.O. No. 6
	" 16th	Training & working parties.	
	" 17th	do.	
	" 18th	do. Batt. killed & shelled Casualties 2 O.R. Killed	
	" 19th	and 2 O.R. wounded.	

Army Form C. 2118.

WAR DIARY
or
INTELLIGENCE SUMMARY.
(Erase heading not required.)

Instructions regarding War Diaries and Intelligence Summaries are contained in F.S. Regs., Part II. and the Staff Manual respectively. Title pages will be prepared in manuscript.

Hour, Date, Place	Summary of Events and Information	Remarks and references to Appendices
FREMICOURT. May 20th.	Church Parade; Divisional funeral and Band attends.	Sheet 57c.
do. May 21st	Training.	
Transfer to MORCHIES. May 22nd	Batt. relieved 1/5th R. Warwick Regt. as Batt. in Brigade Res. near MORCHIES. (Sheet 57c.)	Ref. O.O. No. 7
do. May 23rd	Holding trenches.	
do. 24th	do.	
do. 25th	do.	
do. 26th	do.	
do. 27th	do.	
do. 28th	do. Two other ranks gassed on duty.	
do. 29th	do.	
BEAUMETZ-MORCHIES 30th June	Batt. relieved by 1/5th R. Warwick Regt. and later over BEAUMETZ-MORCHIES line from 1/7th the Worc. Regt. Two Companies at BEUGNY. (Sheet 57c.)	Ref. O.O. No. 8.
do. 31st	Two Coys. in trenches, 2 Coys. at BEUGNY.	

Ration Strength 31/5/17
Officers: 31
O.R.: 733

Casualties
O.R.: 2 Killed
3 Wounded

L/C Bugman C/Sgt ...
Comdg. 1/6th Bn. Glouc. Regiment.

(73989) W4141—463. 400,000. 9/14. H.&J.Ltd. Forms/C. 2118/10.

1/6th Bn. Gloucester Regt. Copy No 1
Battn. Operation Order No. 2.

I. The Battn. will be relieved by the 6th Lancs. Fusiliers tomorrow night 2nd inst.

II. Coys. will be relieved as under:-
"A" Coy. 6th Glouc. by "D" Coy. 6th Lancs. Fus.
  B   "   "   "   B   "   "   "
  C   "   "   "   C   "   "   "
  D   "   "   "   A   "   "   "

III. Guides on the scale of 1 per Coy. H.Q. and 1 per platoon will be at Battn. H.Q. at 8.30pm tomorrow. Those guides for the front line Coys. will be sent to the Support Coy. LEMPIRE tonight and they will be accommodated there by O.C. "D" Coy. until tomorrow evening.
O.C. "D" Coy. will also send an officer to Battn. H.Q. at 8.30 pm tomorrow night to take charge of all guides.

IV. After relief the Battn. will move to VILLERS FAUCON, each platoon moving independently when relieved.
Lieut. Score, "B" Coy. C.Q.M.S's and L. Cpl. WEBBER will act as advanced party and will report to the Town Major, VILLERS FAUCON at 3pm tomorrow.

V. Lewis Gun Limbers and transport for Officers' Mess etc. will be at the cross roads RONSSOY, F.15.d.88 by 9.45 pm. Coy. Commanders' horses will be at the crater at entrance to RONSSOY, F.21.c.49 – 'D' Coy. at 10 pm, and for 'B' & 'C' at 11 pm.

VI Relief complete will be reported to Battn. H.Q. by the code word – BON.

VII Separate orders have been issued to Transport Officer & Q.M.

VIII Trench Stores will be handed over to the incoming unit.

All Battn. Stores eg. VERY PISTOLS Water Tins etc. will be brought out.

A receipt will be obtained of all stores handed over and a copy forwarded to Battn. H.Q.

W.H. Coombs
Lieut & A/Adjt.
for O.C. 1/6th Glouc. Regt.

Issued at 1/5/17

Copies 1 & 2 – War Diary
   " 3 - 6 – Coys.
   " 7 – Q.M. & T.O. for information
   " 8 – R.S.M.

1/6th Bn. Gloucestershire Regiment.

Battalion Operation Order No.3   3rd May, 1917.

Ref. Sheet 62C - 1/40,000

1. MOVE.   The Battalion will move into Camp at BUIRE tomorrow, 4th instant.

2. MARCH.   The Battalion will move by platoons at 100 yards interval. Dress: marching order.
           When marching into or out of billets or camps, or marching at attention, steel helmets will be worn. When marching at ease, caps may be worn and helmets carried.
           Order of march :-
           Hdqrs. "A" "B" "C" "D" Transport
Leading platoon of "A" Company will pass the crater at E.28.a.8.5 at 8 am. Route: ROISEL - TINCOURT. Camp will be pitched on arrival.

3. TRANSPORT.   Transport not coming to VILLERS FAUCON, will join the Battalion on line of march at ROISEL.
           Blankets rolled in bundles of ten will be dumped near the Church, VILLERS FAUCON at 7 am.
           Officers' valises and mess stores will be dumped near the Church, VILLERS FAUCON, ready for loading at 7-30 am.
           Medical cart will be at the Medical Room at 7 am.
           Pioneers will load limbers etc.
           Cooker horses will report to Companies at 7-30 am
Water carts filled, will follow the Battalion.
           Lewis Guns loaded on limbers today, will move under arrangements of T.O.
           Company Commanders' chargers will report to Coys. at 7-45 am., Hdqrs. chargers at 8 am.

(Sgd) C.H. Coombs
3/5/17.   Lieut. & A/Adjt.

1/6th Bn. Gloucestershire Regiment.

Battalion Operation Order No.4   11th May, 1917.

1. MOVE. The Battalion will move to PERONNE tomorrow 12th instant.

2. ORDER OF MARCH. "A" "B" "C" "D" "Hdqrs."

3. STARTING POINT. "A" Company will pass starting point : Hdqrs. Mess at 6 pm. Companies will proceed at intervals of 200 yards. Transport will move 200 yards in rear of Hdqrs.

4. ROUTE. Via DOINGT - Fby. de BRETAGNE.

5. STORES. Mess Stores and Officers' valises will be outside Hdqrs. Mess ready for loading at 5 pm.

6. LEWIS GUNS. Lewis Gun Limbers and Medical Cart will be at the Camp for loading at 5 pm. Officers' chargers at 5-30 pm

11/5/17.

Rupman Lieut. & A/Adjt.

1/6th Bn. Gloucestershire Regiment.

Battalion Operation Order No.5   12th May, 1917.

---

1. **MOVE.** The Battalion will move to COMBLES tomorrow.

2. **PARADE.** The Battalion will parade in column of route facing East at 4-30 am, head of column at PERONNE Town Hall. Order of march :-

    "Hdqrs."   "C"   "D"   "B"   "A"

    Companies to move at an interval of 100 yards.

3. **MESS STORES.** Mess stores and Officers' valises of "A" "B" & "C" Coys. to be dumped outside the Q.M.Stores at 3-45 am. "D" Coys. & Hdqrs. to be outside Hdqrs. Mess at 3-45 am.

4. **BILLETING PARTY.** 1 N.C.O. per Company and one each from Hdqrs. & Q.M.Stores will remain and report to Lieut. Pope outside the Town Major's Office, The Square, PERONNE, at 5-15 am.

12/5/17.   *[signature]* Lieut. & A/Adjt.

1/6th Bn. Gloucestershire Regiment.

Battalion Operation Order No.6.   13th May 1917.

1. MOVE.   The Battalion will move to FREMICOURT tomorrow 14th instant.

2. ROUTE.   FREGICOURT - SAILLY SAILLISEL - LE TRANSLOY - BAPAUME.

3. PARADE.   Companies will parade at 5 am in front of Company billets.

4. ORDER OF MARCH.
   "Hdqrs."   "D"   "C"   "A"   "B"

   Interval between Companies : 100 yards, Transport 200 yards in rear of "B" Company.

5. STORES.   Officers' kits and mess stores will be outside the Q.M.Stores at 4-30 am.

6. BILLETING PARTY.
   1 N.C.O. per Company, 1 N.C.O. from Q.M.Stores, and the Battalion Interpreter will report to Lieut.Pope outside Battalion Hdqrs. at 4-15 am.

7. MARCH DISCIPLINE.
   No cigarettes will be smoked except during halts.

                                    Lieut. & A/Adjt.

13/5/17.

1/6th Bn. Gloucestershire Regiment.

Battalion Operation Order No.7.   22nd May, 1917.

---

1. **RELIEF.** The Battalion will relieve the 1/5th Royal Warwickshire Regiment in the trenches tonight.

2. **DISPOSITIONS.** Companies will take over as under :-

    "A" Coy. from "A" Coy. 1/5th R.Warwicks.
    "B" Coy. from "B" Coy.   do.
    "C" Coy. from "C" Coy.   do.
    "D" Coy. from "D" Coy.   do.

3. **MOVE.** The Battalion will move by platoons at 100 yards interval, in the following order :-

    "Hdqrs." "D" "A" "C" "B"

    Route: Via BAPAUME - CAMBRAI main road. Headquarters will move off at 8-10 pm.

4. **GUIDES.** One guide per platoon and two guides for Headquarters will be at road junction I.16.c.9.0. at 9 pm.

5. **SIGNALLERS.** Signallers for Company Stations will report to Company Commanders before the Battalion leaves FREMICOURT.

6. **STORES.** One limber per Company will report at Company Hdqrs. at 8 pm. for carrying Lewis Guns and Mess Stores. Two Lewis Gunners and one batman will accompany each limber.
    One limber will report at Battalion Headquarters at 8 pm.

7. Grooms for Officers' chargers will be at road junction I.16.c.9.0. at 9 pm.

8. **COOKERS.** "D" Coys. cooker will go up filled. Battalion Water Carts will fill "A" "B" & "C" Coys. cooker dixies after arrival at trenches. All small oval dixies on Company charge will be taken up.

22/5/17.   [signature] Lieut. & Adjt.

NOTICE.

Extract from Brigade Orders -

"In some cases it may be impossible to quite complete all reliefs before dawn. Should this be the case, parties must be ordered to remain where they are at dawn until it is possible for them to get up the following night".

"It is absolutely necessary to avoid all movement during the hours of daylight".

-------oOo-------

1/6th Bn. Gloucestershire Regiment.

Battalion Operation Order No.8.   30th May, 1917.

Ref. Map 57C N.E. 1/20,000

1. **RELIEF.** The Battalion will be relieved on the night of the 30/31st May by the 1/5th Royal Warwick Regiment.

2. **MOVE.** On relief the Battalion will move and take over the defence of the MORCHIES - BEAUMETZ line from the 1/7th Worcester Regiment.

3. **DISPOSITIONS.** Reference Defence Scheme issued to Companies, the dispositions will be as under -

    "A" Coy. - Left Front Coy.
    "B" Coy. - Right   "   "
    "C" Coy. - Battalion Reserve
    "D" Coy. -   "   "

4. **GUIDES.** One guide per platoon of "A" "B" & "C" Coys. will be ready at Company Hdqrs. to take the incoming platoons to their shelters.
    Company relieving forward Company, will march direct to posts under their own guides.
    Probable time of relief : 10 pm.

5. O's C. "A" & "B" Companies will send 1 Officer per Company and 1 other rank per platoon at 6 pm to take over the shelters etc.
    Similar parties from "C" & "D" Companies will be at BEUGNY by 4-30 pm.
    These parties must show Transport where to unload.
    O.C. "B" Company will have a guide at BEETROOT FACTORY at 9 pm to guide transport to "B" Company Hdqrs.

6. O's C. the Right & Left Front Companies will send sufficient N.C.O's to reconnoitre the posts of the defensive line.

7. One water cart will remain at BEUGNY for the Companies in Battalion Reserve, and one water cart will visit the Right & Left Front Coy. Hdqrs. at 10 pm each night to fill dixies and 20 petrol tins per Company.

8. The petrol tins distributed to Companies on the night 29/30th May will be handed over to the 1/5th R.Warwick Regt.

9. **TRENCH STORES ETC.**
    S.A.A., Bombs etc. will be handed over as trench stores, and all work in progress will be handed over.

10. The packs of "D" Company will be taken to BEUGNY.

30/5/17.   Lieut. & Adjt.

Confidential

Vol 27

War Diary
of
1/6th Bn the Gloucestershire Regt (T.F.)

1st June to 30th June 1914

(VOL. XXVII)

L. Abram
27. R
7 rmt

Army Form C. 2118.

WAR DIARY
INTELLIGENCE SUMMARY.
(Erase heading not required.)

1/6th GLOUCESTER REGMT.
JUNE 1917.

Instructions regarding War Diaries and Intelligence Summaries are contained in F.S. Regs., Part II. and the Staff Manual respectively. Title pages will be prepared in manuscript.

Hour, Date, Place		Summary of Events and Information	Remarks and references to Appendices
JUNE 1st 1917.	MORCHIES.	Battn. holding BEAUMETZ – MORCHIES line with 2 Coy. at BEUGNY. Battn. H.Qrs. at I.14.6.5. (Sheet 57C. N.W.)	
2nd.	ditto	ditto	
3rd.	ditto	ditto	
4th.	ditto	ditto. Lt.-Col. H. St.G. Schomberg rejoined from hospital.	
5th.	ditto	ditto. 2/Lt. C.W. Kingdom joined for duty. Div. Commander awarded K.C.B.	
6th.	Trenches.	Battn. relieved 1/8th R. Warwick Regt. in Left. Front Battn. Sector. Left Brigade. Relief complete 2 a.m. 7/6/17. Front D.20.a–D.22.d. Two Coys. holding front line system, 2 Coy. + Batt. H.Qrs in AGNICOURT – DOIGNES road.	Ref. O.O. No 9. (Ref. Sheet 57C. M.E./20,000)
7th – 11th.	do.	Battn. holding line opposite PRONVILLE. Hot, quiet. Work wiring.	
11th.	do.	Capt. J.M. LOWICK rejoined Battn.	
12th.	do.	Holding same line. Very hot, very quiet.	
13th.	do.	do	
14th.	do.	Relieved by 1/8th R. Warwick Regt. and to Camp at FREMICOURT. Relief Complete 2.30 a.m. 15/6/17.	
15th. FREMICOURT.		Battn cleaning up. 30 O.R. joined for duty. Reinforcement 1/4 O.B.R. arrived.	
16th.	do.	Battn. + training.	
17th.	do.	Church parade – 2 Coy. on working party.	
18th.	do.	Training. Batt. Field Practice.	
19th – 22nd.	do.	Training. Rifle Range notified.	
23rd.	Trenches.	Battn. relieved 1/5 R. Warwick Regt. in Support Battn. Left Brigade. One Coy. holding Reserve Line on Rd. LAGNICOURT – DOIGNES road. Remainder Battn. on LAGNICOURT – BEAUMETZ road. Relief complete 1 a.m. 24/6/17. 2/Lt. SODSON killed.	
24th – 30th.	do.	Battn. holding same support position. 29/6/17.	

NOTES. Fine weather throughout the month. Health uniformly excellent. Casualties. 1 Officer killed. 1 O.R. killed. 7 O.R. wounded.

Ref. O.O. No. 10.
Ref. O.O. No. 11.
O.O. No. 12.

Ration Strength 30/6/17
26 Officers
710 O.R.
On Command { 6 Officers, 63 O.R. }

H. St.G. Schomberg Lieut. Col.
Comdg. 1/6 Gloucester Regt.

1/6th Bn. Gloucestershire Regiment.

Battalion Operation Order No. 9.   6th June, 1917.

1. **RELIEF.**
   The Battalion will take over trenches from 1/8th Royal Warwickshire Regiment tonight.

2. **DISPOSITIONS.**
   "B" Coy. will take over Right Front area from "C" Coy. R.W.Rs
   "C" Coy.   "   "   "   Left   "   "   " "D" Coy.   "
   "A" Coy.   "   "   "   Right Res. "   "   " "A" Coy. "
   "D" Coy.   "   "   "   Left Res. "   "   " "B" Coy. "

3. **GUIDES.**
   Guides on the scale of 1 per platoon, 1 for each Company Hdqrs., and 1 for Battalion Headquarters will be at D.25.d.7.0. at 10-15 pm.

4. **ORDER OF MARCH.**
   The Battalion will move as under:-
   Hdqrs., "B" Coy. plus 1 platoon of "A" Coy.,
   "C" Coy. plus 1 platoon of "D" Coy.
   "A"   "D"
   Headquarters will move off at 9-30 pm. Distance between platoons: 100 yards.

5. **OFFICERS' VALISES ETC.** of & & Coy
   Officers' valises, surplus mess stores, and all empty petrol tins of "C" & "D" Companies will be dumped at Battalion Headquarters by 8-45 pm.
   Small oval dixies will be returned to the Quartermaster on cookers.

6. **RATIONS.**
   Rations of "A" & "B" Companies will be taken on the man. Rations of "C" & "D" Companies will be taken direct to trenches by transport.
   Two cooks per Company will proceed to trenches with their Company.

7. **TRANSPORT.**
   1 limber per Company will be provided for carrying mess stores and Lewis Guns. These will be at Company Hdqrs. as soon after dark as possible.

8. **BATTALION HEADQUARTERS.**
   Battalion Headquarters will be at D.26.c.4.1.

9. **CODE.**
   Code word for "RELIEF COMPLETE" will be "RATS"

6/6/17.   F S Rymon Lieut. & Adjt.

1/8th Bn. Gloucestershire Regt.

Battalion Operation Order No.10.   14th June, 1917.

---

1. **RELIEF.** The Battalion will be relieved tonight 14/15th by the 1/8th Royal Warwickshire Regiment and will proceed to billets at FREMICOURT.

2. **GUIDES.** O's C. "A" & "D" Companies will have 1 guide per platoon ~~and Company Hdqrs~~. at Company Hdqrs. at 10-15 pm to guide relieving platoons to front posts and support positions. No guides will be required by reliefs of "C" & "B" Companies.

3. **MOVE.** Companies will maintain distances of 100 yds. between platoons until West of BEUGNY. Platoons attached to Front Companies will move under orders of Front Company Commanders.

4. **BILLETS.** Coy.Q.M.Serjts. will take over billets for their respectively Companies.

5. **TRANSPORT.** 1 limber per Company and 1 for Headquarters will report at 10-30 pm to take back Lewis Guns and Mess Stores.

6. **PETROL TINS.** All petrol tins will be collected at Company Hdqrs. and handed over to Warwick limbers for return.

7. **HANDING OVER.** All trench stores, Intelligence and work in progress will be handed over to relieving unit. Company Commanders will render to this Office by 10-30 pm, lists of all trench stores handed over.

8. **CHARGERS.** Company Officers' chargers will be at CHAUFFOURS WOOD at 11-30 pm.

9. **BATHS.** Baths at HAPLINCOURT are allotted to "D" Company from 3 pm - 5 pm tomorrow, 15th instant.

10. **CODE.** Code word for Relief Complete - EASY.

14/6/17.   [signature] Lieut. & Adjt.

1/6th Bn. Gloucestershire Regiment.

Battalion Operation Order No.11.   17th June, 1917.

Ref. Map 57C - 1/40,000

PRACTICE

1. The enemy has taken our Support line running along LEBUCQUIERE - FREMICOURT with the exception of posts at LEBUCQUIERE, DELSAUX Farm & FREMICOURT which are still holding out.

   He is attacking our Reserve line which runs from VELU, North of SUSSEX Camp to BANCOURT.

2. The Brigade will defeat his attack on the Reserve line and will retake the Support line.

3. The 1/6th Gloucester Regt. will move as the Left Battalion in front line of the Brigade which has three Battalions in the front line.

4. OBJECTIVES.
   (1) To drive back the enemy who are attacking our Reserve line in I.32.d.
   (2) Retake Support line between point 50 yards East of cross roads in I.27.a.10. and WATER TOWER about I.26.b.60.

5. At 7-30 am in conjunction with Battalion on our right, the Battalion will advance as follows :-

   "A" Company on the Right, "B" Company on the Left, "D" Company will send forward one platoon to form left flank guard.
   "C" Company and the remainder of "D" Company, will form Battalion Reserve in valley O.2.b.& d.
   Battalion Headquarters will be at cross roads O.2.b.08.

   Battalion Signalling Officer will arrange for Signal communication with attacking Companies & Battalion on our Right.

   Dressing Station: Cross roads O.2.b.08.
   Reserve Ammunition in valley O.2.b.& d.

                                             Lieut.Col.,
17/6/17.   Comdg. 1/6th Bn. Gloucestershire Rgt.

            Copy No.1 - File.
                 2   - 144 Brigade Hdqrs.
                 3-6   - Companies

1/6th Bn. Gloucestershire Regiment.

Battalion Operation Order No.12.   23rd June, 1917.

1. **RELIEF.**   The Battalion will relieve the 1/6th Royal Warwickshire Regiment tonight.

2. **DISPOSITIONS.**   The Battalion will take over as under –

   C Coy will relieve D Coy 1/6 R.W. in front Coy Sector.
   A Coy   "   "   A Coy "   " in Left Support
   B Coy   "   "   B Coy "   " in Right Support
   D Coy   "   "   C Coy "   " in Centre Support

3. **MOVE.**   The Battalion will move in the following order :–
   "C"   "Hdqrs"   "A"   "B"   "D"

   Dress: marching order.   Rations for tomorrow will be carried on the man.   Distance of 100 yards between platoons will be maintained.   "C" Company will move off at 8-45 pm.

4. **GUIDES.**   Post Guides for "C" Company and 1 guide for "C" Coy. Hdqrs. will be at Farm J.8.c.7.3. at 10 pm.
   Headquarters, "A" "B" & "D" Companies will proceed to their respective destinations under their own arrangements.

5. **TRANSPORT.**   1 limber per Company and 1 for Headquarters will be at the Camp at 8-15 pm
   Officers' chargers will be at the Camp at 8-30 pm.

6. **COOKERS.**   Cookers of "B" "C" & "D" Companies will be taken into trenches.
   O.C. "A" Company will arrange to take up requisite cooks and dixies for making tea.

7. **BAND.**   Band personnel will proceed to trenches with Companies.

8. **CODE.**   Code word for "Relief Complete" – PEACH.

F.D. Rupman Lieut. & Adjt.

Confidential

Vol 28

War Diary
of
16th Bn. Gloucestershire Regt. (TF)

1st July to 31st July 1917

(Vol XXVIII)

Army Form C. 2118.

WAR DIARY
INTELLIGENCE SUMMARY.
(Erase heading not required.)

1/6th GLOUCESTER REGT
JULY 1917.

Instructions regarding War Diaries and Intelligence Summaries are contained in F.S. Regs., Part II. and the Staff Manual respectively. Title pages will be prepared in manuscript.

Hour, Date, Place		Summary of Events and Information	Remarks and references to Appendices
July 1st 1917.	Trenches.	Batt'n in support. Left Brigade Sector. 1 Company holding line on LAGNICOURT - DOIGNES Rd. rest of Batt'n in LAGNICOURT - BEAUMETZ road.	Ref Sheet 57° N.W.
2nd	Do.	Relieved by 7th Kings Shropshire L.I. Relief complete 12.20am 3/7/17.	O.O. No 13.
3rd	BEUGNY.	Batt'n moved back to camp at BEUGNY. At 2 p.m. Batt'n moved via BAPAUME to ACHIET-LE-PETIT. Intense heat. 30 cases admitted to F.A. en route. Batt'n in camp ACHIET-LE-PETIT at 6 p.m.	O.O. No 14. Ref Sheet 57c
4th	ACHIET-LE-PETIT		
5th	HENDECOURT	Batt'n moved from ACHIET-LE-PETIT to HENDECOURT. Started from allowed 11.15 p.m. Ref. LENS 11. 1/100,000.	D.O. No 15.
6th	Do.	In Camp. training.	
7th	Do.	In Camp. training. Major W. ADAM posted to command of 1/6 GLOUC. REGT. Major P. PICKFORD, Ox & Bucks L.I. joined Batt'n for duty as 2nd in command.	
8th	Do.	Divisional Tactical Exercise by 144 Bde. over old trench system MONCHY-AU-BOIS. O.O's verbal.	Ref. Sheets 51° S.E. 51° N.E.
9th	Do.	(Sunday) Divine Services in Camp	
10th	Do.	In Camp training	
11th	Do.	In Camp training	
12th	Do.	In Camp training	
13th	Do.	In Camp training. Draft of 153 O.R's arrived.	
14th	Do.	In Camp training. Inoculation.	
15th	Do.	In Camp training.	
16th	Do.	(Sunday) Divine Services in Camp	
17th	Do.	Divisional Tactical Exercise by 144 Bde. over old trench system MONCHY-AU-BOIS. In Camp training	O.O. No 16. Ref Sheets 51c S.E. 51° N.E.

(CONTINUED)

Army Form C. 2118.

WAR DIARY (CONTINUED) 1/6th GLOUCESTER REGT.
INTELLIGENCE SUMMARY.
JULY 1917.

(Erase heading not required.)

Instructions regarding War Diaries and Intelligence Summaries are contained in F.S. Regs., Part II. and the Staff Manual respectively. Title pages will be prepared in manuscript.

Hour, Date, Place	Summary of Events and Information	Remarks and references to Appendices
JULY 18th HENDECOURT	In Camp. Training.	
19th Do.	In Camp. Training.	
20th Do.	Batt. marched to billets vacated by 1/4 R. Wn. R. at BIENVILLERS. Started 2.30pm. All in 5.30pm.	O.O. No. 17. Ref. Sheet LENS 11.
21st BIENVILLERS	In Billets	Ref. Sheet LENS 11
22nd Do.	Batt. paraded 3am. + marched to SAULTY-LABRET Stn. arriving 5am. Batt. + transport entrained at 7am. + detrained at HOPOUTRE 4pm. Batt. marched to billets in POPERINGHE, all in 9pm. Transport brigaded near HOPOUTRE Stn.	D.O. No. 18. Ref. Sheet HAZEBROUCK 5A
23rd POPERINGHE	Batt. moved at 6.30pm to camp near ST. JANS-TER-BIEZEN. Transport remained at HOPOUTRE. Pitched on arrival.	Ref. Sheet HAZEBROUCK 5A
24th 25th 26th ST JANS-TER-BIEZEN 27th 28th	Training in Camp	Casualties:- 1 O.R. Died 1 O.R. Died of wounds Ration Strength OFFICERS 32 O RANKS 858
27th	Capt D.H. HARTOG. M.C. joined for duty.	
29th 30th	Capt E.W. TAME joined for duty.	Ambulances, leave etc.
29th	A 29 started 8am.	O.O. No. 19. OFFICERS 6 O. RANKS 90
31st ST JANS-TER-BIEZEN.	Marched to camp in A. started 8am.	Ref Sheet 28 + HAZEBROUCK 5A

A.J. Whinney
Lieut. Col.
comndg. 1/6th Bat. Gloucestershire Regiment

1/6th Bn. Gloucestershire Regiment.

Battalion Operation Order No.14. - 2nd July, 1917.

1. MOVE. The Battalion will move to ACHIET-LE-PETIT area tomorrow.

2. PARADE. Companies will parade in BEUGNY Camp at 1-45 pm tomorrow.

3. MARCH. The Battalion will move off at 2 pm in the following order :-

   "Hdqrs" "A" "B" "C" "D"

   Battalion Band will march in rear of "A" Company. Distance of 200 yards will be maintained between Companies and sections of Transport.
   Route: Via BAPAUME and ACHIET-LE-GRAND.

4. BILLETING PARTY.
   One N.C.O. per Company and one from Headquarters will report to Lieut.W.J.H.POPE at Battalion Headquarters BEUGNY Camp, at 10-45 am. This party will proceed on bicycles.

5. MESS STORES & VALISES.
   Mess Stores and valises will be outside Company Hdqrs., BEUGNY Camp, ready for loading at 1 pm.

6. MARCH DISCIPLINE.
   Strict march discipline will be observed on the march.

2/7/17.   [signature] Lieut. & Adjt.

1/6th Bn. Gloucestershire Regiment.

Battalion Operation Order No.15.   3rd July, 1917.

═══

Ref. Sheet LENS II

1. **MOVE.** The Battalion will move to HENDECOURT tomorrow 4th instant.

2. **PARADE.** The Battalion will parade at 7 am and will move off in the following order:-

    Hdqrs. Band, "B" "C" "D" "A" Transport

    200 yards will be maintained between Companies and sections of Transport.

3. **ROUTE.** Via ABLAINZEVELLE - AYETTE.

4. **BILLETING PARTY.** 1 N.C.O. per Company, Headquarters, Q.M.Stores & Transport will report to Lieut. W.H. Coombs at Battalion Headquarters at 6-30 am. They will proceed on bicycles.

5. **MESS STORES.** Mess Stores and Officers' valises will be ready to load at 6-15 am.

6. O.C. "D" Company will detail an Officer to march in rear of the Battalion and to collect and bring on stragglers.

3/7/17.   [signature] Lieut. & Adjt.,

1/5th Bn. Gloucestershire Regiment.

DIVISIONAL TACTICAL EXERCISE.   OPERATION ORDER NO. 16.

15th July, 1917.

Ref: Sheets 51C E.E.
     57D N.E.

1. The Battalion will march tomorrow 16th inst. to BIENVILLERS, where it will breakfast prior to doing a Tactical Exercise.

2. PARADE.
    The Battalion will parade in column of route facing East on the road outside Camp at 4-25 am. Order of march :-

        Hdqrs. "D" "C" "A" "B"

    Head of column to be outside the Orderly Room. Dress: Fighting order with haversack rations. The Battalion will parade at full strength except -

    (a) Men excused duty by Medical Officer at tonight's sick parade.

    (b) One man of "D" Coy. to look after Company Messes, 1 for Headquarters, 1 for Q.M.Stores and 2 Regimental Police.

3. TRANSPORT.
    Battalion Transport will move Brigaded in rear, except the following, which will accompany the Battalion -

        Mess Cart, Water Carts, Cookers.

15/7/17.   A E Rayner Lieut. & Adjt.

                    N O T E.

    At Tactical Exercise, men waving flags indicate M.G's in action.

1/6th Bn. Gloucestershire Regiment.

Battalion Operation Order No.17.   20th July, 1917.

===

1. **MOVE.**   The Battalion will move to BIENVILLERS this afternoon.

2. **PARADE.**   The Battalion will parade in column of route facing West, on the road through Camp at 3 pm. Order of march -

    Hdqrs. "A" "B" Band "C" "D"

    Head of column opposite Orderly Room.

3. **SURPLUS STORES & KITS.**
    All surplus mess stores and kits which will not be required before entraining on the 22nd, will be dumped outside the Guard Room by 1-30 pm. A lorry will take these direct to entraining station.

4. **OTHER STORES & OFFICERS' VALISES.**
    Other stores and Officers' valises will be outside Headquarters by 1-30 pm. Pioneers will load.

5. **LEWIS GUNS.**
    Lewis Gun limbers will be at the Camp for loading at 2-30 pm.

6. **OFFICERS' CHARGERS.**
    Officers' chargers will be at the Camp at 2-45 pm.

7. **BIVOUAC SHEETS.**
    "A" & "B" Companies will each hand over 15 bivouac sheets to Town Major at Office behind Orderly Room by 1 pm.
    "C" & "D" Companies will each dump 14 bivouac sheets outside Battalion Headquarters by 12 noon today.

20/7/17.   Lieut. & Adjt.

All Coy., T.O, & Q. M.

O.O. No. 18

Battn. will move to SAULTY-LABRET entraining Station tomorrow morning. Battn. will arrive at Station 4.59 a.m. Train will move off 5.9 a.m.

1. PARADE. Battn. will parade in column of route facing EAST on the Battn. H-Qrs-Church road at 2.55 a.m. Head of column at Church.

2. Order of March H.Qrs, C, D, Band, A, B.

3. VALISES & MESS STORES will be at Q. Mstr. Stores at 2 a.m.

4. WATER BOTTLES will be filled before parade.

F.W. Tryman Lt/Adjt
21/7/17.

1/6th Bn. Gloucestershire Regiment.

Battalion Operation Order No.19.   30th July, 1917.

Reference Sheet HAZEBROUCK - 1/100,000
              "   28 - 1/20,000

1. **MOVE.** The Battalion will move to "C" Brigade Group Area in A.29 tomorrow 31st July.
   Route: POPERINGHE - POPERINGHE ELVERDINGHE Road and PLANK Road.

2. **CAMP.** The Camp will be struck and all tents and tarpaulins stacked by road outside Camp entrance by 7-30 am.

3. **PARADE.** Companies will parade independently in Camp at 8-25 am. Order of march :-

   Hdqrs. "D" "C" Band "A" "B"

   Distance between Companies 200 yards.

4. **STORES.** All mess stores and valises will be on site of Guard Tent at 7-45 am. Pioneers will load.

5. **LEWIS GUNS.** Lewis Guns will be loaded on limbers tonight.

6. Officers' chargers will be at Camp at 8-20 am.
   Cookers will accompany Companies.

30/7/17.   Lieut. & Adjt.

War Diary
of
1/6th the Gloucestershire Regt. T.F.

From 1/8/14 to 31/8/14

(VOL. XXIX)

29 R

Army Form C. 2118.

WAR DIARY
or
INTELLIGENCE SUMMARY.

(Erase heading not required.)

1/6th Bn. GLOUC. REGT.

AUGUST. 1917.

Instructions regarding War Diaries and Intelligence Summaries are contained in F.S. Regs., Part II. and the Staff Manual respectively. Title pages will be prepared in manuscript.

Hour, Date, Place		Summary of Events and Information	Remarks and references to Appendices
August.	1st CAMP. A.29.d.	In camp	Sheet 28 N.W.
	2nd Do.	In camp	
	3rd Do.	In camp	
	4th Do.	In camp	
	5th Do.	In camp	
	6th Do.	Batt" moved at 9 a.m. to DAMBRE CAMP (B)	
	7th DAMBRE CAMP	In camp	O.O. No. 20. Ref Sheet 28 N.W.
	8th Do.	Batt" relieved 1/4 Ox. + Bucks in reserve trenches	O.O. No. 21. Ref Sheet 28 N.W.
	9th TRENCHES.	In reserve trenches	
	10th Do.	Relieved 1/4th GLOUC. REGT. in left Batt"+ sector of front line	O.O. No. 22. Ref Sheet 28 N.W.
	11th Do.	In front line trenches. O.O. received from Brigade for attack on night 12th/13th Intention - to establish a line of posts at least 150 yds East of the STEEN BEEK. A + C Coys ordered to attack.	O.O. No. 23. Ref Sheet 28 N.W.
	12th Do.	Readjustment of Coys in the line preparatory to attack. In front line trenches. Operations cancelled.	
	13th Do.	Relieved by 1/4th GLOUCS + moved down into support. 2 Coys in O.O.1.	O.O. No. 24. Ref Sheet 28 N.W.
	14th In Support.	2 Coys on CANAL BANK. H + 2 Coys in O.O.1. moved back to CANAL BANK.	
	15th Do.	Batt" moved back to REIGERSBERG CAMP.	
	16th REIGERSBERG	Batt" + 2 Coys moved up to CANAL BANK.	
	17th CANAL BANK	H.Qrs. + 2 Coys moved up to CANAL BANK. Relieved 8th WORC. REGT. in support trenches. O.O.1.	O.O. No. 25. Ref Sheet 28 N.W.
	18th In Support	H.Qrs + 2 Coys moved back to CANAL BANK.	O.O. No. 26. Ref Sheet 28 N.W.
	19th Do.	CANAL BANK - O.O.1.	

(CONTINUED).

Army Form C. 2118.

WAR DIARY
or
INTELLIGENCE SUMMARY (CONTD.)

(Erase heading not required.)

1/6 Bn. GLOUC. REGT.

AUGUST 1917

Instructions regarding War Diaries and Intelligence Summaries are contained in F.S. Regs., Part II. and the Staff Manual respectively. Title pages will be prepared in manuscript.

Hour, Date, Place		Summary of Events and Information	Remarks and references to Appendices
August 20th	In Support. Front trenches	Relieved 6 WORCS. in front line in front line trenches.	O.O. No. 27. Ref Sheet 28 N.W.
21st			
22nd	Do.	Operations in accordance with attached	O.O. No. 28. Ref Sheets POPERINGHE & 28 N.W.
23rd	Do.	Relieved by 4th GLOUCS. Battn moved back to CANAL BANK	O.O. No. 29. Ref Sheet 28 N.W.
24th	CANAL BANK.	Battn moved to REIGERSBERG CAMP	O.O. No. 30. Ref Sheet 28 N.W.
25th	REIGERSBERG.	in camp.	
26th	Do.	H.Qrs + 2 Coys moved to CANAL BANK. O.G.I.	
27th	In Support.	in trenches O.G.I. Attack by Division. Very wet day.	
28th	Do.	Left O.G.I. at 5am. + moved back to DAMBRE CAMP.	
29th	DAMBRE CAMP.	Left camp 9.40am. + marched to SCHOOL CAMP near ST. JAN-TER-BIEZEN.	O.O. No. 31. Ref Sheets 28. N.W. + HAZEBROUCK 5A
		Bomb party rejoined. Draft of 2 Officers + 133 O.R's arrived.	
30th	ST. JAN-TER-BIEZEN	on SCHOOL CAMP.	
31st	Do.	Do.	

Casualties during month
	Offs.	O.R's
Killed	1	20
Died of Wounds		1
Wounded	5	89
Gassed		9
Missing		
	6	119

Drafts received during month
2 Offs. 133 O.R's.

Ration Strength
28 Offs. 734 O.R's

[signature] Major.

comdg 1/6th Bn. Gloucestershire Regiment

1/5th Bn. Gloucestershire Regiment.

Battalion Operation Order No.30.   5th August, 1917.

Ref. Sheet BELGIUM, 28 N.W.

1. **MOVE.** The Battalion will move tomorrow 6th inst. to DAMBRE CAMP (H). Route: Chemin Militaire and VLAMERTINGHE - ELVERDINGHE Road.

2. **PARADE.** Companies will parade independently on open space near Battalion Guard Tent at 9 am. Dress: marching order. Order of march :-

    H'qrs. "D" "B" "C" "A"

    Distance between Companies : 200 yards.

3. **MESSES.** Mess stores and valises will be outside the Q.M.Stores at 9 am. Pioneers will load.

4. **LEWIS GUNS.** Lewis Guns will be loaded on limbers tonight.

5. Officers' chargers will be at the Camp at 8-45 am.

6. **REMR.** Personnel detailed for Training Camp, ST. JAN-TER-BIEZEN will remain in present Camp. Further orders will be issued.

5/8/17.   [signature] Lieut. & Adjt.

1/6th Bn. Gloucestershire Regiment.

Battalion Operation Order No.21.   8th August, 1917.

Ref. Sheet 28 N.W.

1. **RELIEF.** The Battalion will take over Reserve trenches from the 1/4th Ox. & Bucks L.I. tonight.

2. **DISPOSITIONS.**
   "A" Coy. will relieve "A" Coy. 1/4th Ox. & Bucks L.I.
   "B" Coy.   "   "   "B" Coy.   "   "   "   "
   "C" Coy.   "   "   "C" Coy.   "   "   "   "
   "D" Coy.   "   "   "D" Coy.   "   "   "   "
   Battalion Headquarters will be at C.22.a.8.7. (where trench board track crosses O.G.1).

3. **ORDER OF MARCH.**
   Hdqrs. "A" "B" "C" "D"
   The Battalion will be ready to move at 4-45 pm. Distance between platoons 200 yards. Route : CHEMIN MILITAIRE, Bridge 2A and trench board track.

4. **GUIDES.** 1 guide per platoon and 1 per Battalion Hdqrs. will be at junction of trench board track with BOUNDARY ROAD (i.e. near IRISH FARM) at 6-15 pm.

5. **STORES.** Lewis Guns, mess stores, Officers' kits, dixies and rum will be loaded on limbers by 4 pm. They will proceed in advance of Battalion and will offload at junction by trench board track with BUFFS ROAD (i.e. near VIEW Farm)
   Representatives from Companies and Hdqrs. will accompany their respective limbers and Battalion will pick up loads at off-loading point.

6. Officers' chargers will be at Camp at 4-30 pm.

7. All water bottles will be filled before the Battalion moves, and tomorrow's meat ration will be cooked and loaded on Company limbers by 4 pm.

8/8/17.   *F.H. Rageman* Lieut. & Adjt.

1/6th Bn. Gloucestershire Regiment.

Battalion Operation Order No. 22.   10th August, 1917.

Ref. Sheet 28 N.W.

1. **RELIEF.** The Battalion will relieve the 1/4th Gloucestershire Regiment in the Left Front Battalion Sector tonight.

2. **DISPOSITIONS.** Companies will take over as under –
   "A" Coy. from "A" Coy. 1/4th Glouc. Regt.
   "B" Coy.   "   "B" Coy.   "   "   "
   "C" Coy.   "   "C" Coy.   "   "   "
   "D" Coy.   "   "D" Coy.   "   "   "
   O.C. "B" Coy. will attach 1 platoon of "B" Company to be under orders of O.C. "D" Company.

3. **GUIDES.** 1/4th Gloucesters will provide 1 guide per platoon and 1 for Coy. Hdqrs. for each of "A" "C" and "B" Coys. These will be at junction of trench board track with O.G. 1 (50 yards N. of Battalion Headquarters) at 9 pm. "D" Company plus attached platoon of "B" Coy. will relieve in daylight independently.
   O.C. "D" Company will report at Battalion Headquarters at once for instructions.

4. **ORDER OF MARCH.**
   "A" "C" 3 platoons "B"
   Leading platoon of "A" Company will be at guide point at 9 pm, ditto of "C" Coy. at 9-15 pm., ditto for "B" Coy. at 9-30 pm. Distance between platoons 200 yards.

5. **GUIDES FOR 4th GLOUC.** O.C. Companies will detail 1 guide per platoon and 1 for Company Hdqrs. to remain at guide point and guide 4th Glouc. to their positions at our present area.

6. **RATIONS & WATER.** Rations and water for tomorrow will be carried up on the man. Water can only be taken up at night, so Companies must take up tonight as many filled tins as possible.

7. Battalion Headquarters will be in Civilisation Farm with advanced Hdqrs. at C.10.d.6.5.

10/8/17.   _____ Lieut. & Adjt.

1/6th Bn. Gloucestershire Regiment.

Battalion Operation Order No. 24.   13th August, 1917.

==

Ref. Sheet 28 N.W.

1. **RELIEF.**   The Battalion will be relieved in the Left Front Sector by the 1/4th Gloucestershire Regiment tonight, as under :-

   "A" Coy. will be relieved by "A" Coy. 1/4th Glouc.
   "C" Coy.   "   "   "   "   "B" Coy.   "   "
   "D" Coy.   "   "   "   "   "D" Coy.   "   "
   "B" Coy.   "   "   "   "   "C" Coy.   "   "

   "D" Company and one platoon of "B" Company will be relieved independently in daylight. Details of relief to be arranged by O.C. Coys. concerned.

2. **GUIDES.**   One guide per platoon and one for Coy. Hdqrs. will be provided by O.C. "D" Coy. for "A" "B" & 3 platoons of "C" Coy. 4th Glouc.   These guides will conduct 4th Glouc. to Adv. Battalion Hdqrs. where they will wait to guide back relieved platoons of "A" "B" & "C" Coys.

   Guides will be near Support Battalion Hdqrs. at junction of Trench Board Track with O.G.1. at 8-45 pm. tonight under orders detailed by O.C. "D" Company. O's C. "A" "B" & "C" Companies will provide one guide per platoon and 1 per Company Hdqrs. to be at Advanced Battalion Hdqrs. at 9-30 pm. to guide incoming troops to their respective Company Hdqrs. whence they will be guided into position under Coy. arrangements.   All guides will report to 2/Lieut. D.G.Stewart at Adv. Battalion Hdqrs.

3.   On relief, Battalion will proceed as under :-
   (a) "A" & "C" Coys. to CANAL BANK via trench board track leading to Bridge 2A. Here they will be met by billeting representatives from transport lines.
   (b) "B" Coy. to Support Battalion Hdqrs., O.G.1 where they will be met by billeting party from present rear platoon of "B" Coy.

4. **RATIONS.**   Rations for tomorrow will be dumped
   (1) "A" & "C" Coys. at Canal Bank
   (2) "B" & "D" Coys. at junction of ADMIRALS ROAD with BOUNDARY ROAD at 7 am tomorrow morning. Ration parties to fetch.
   "B" & "D" Coys. cooks will come up with their Coys. rations and dixies.

13/8/17.   [signature] Lieut. & Adjt.

1/6th Bn. Gloucestershire Regiment.

Battalion Operation Order No.23.   11th August, 1917.
==

Ref. Sheet 28 N.W.

a. INFORMATION.
   Enemy is holding farm at C.11.b.9.6. and a line of posts from the farm to road at C.5.d.75.50. and probably a line of posts from farm to N. end of ST. JULIEN.

b. INTENTION.
   To drive the enemy back from this line and to establish a line of posts at least 160 yards East of the River STEENBECK.

c. "A" & "C" Companies, 1/6th Bn. Gloucestershire Regt. in conjunction with the 1/7th Bn. R. Warwickshire Regt. on their right will attack enemy's position on night 12/13th under an Artillery barrage as follows :-

   "A" Coy. on the left frontage road REGINA CROSS - TRIANGLE FARM inclusive to Road ALBERTA FARM - Farm at C.11.b.9.6. exclusive.

   "C" Coy. on the right frontage Road ALBERTA FARM - Farm at C.11.b.9.6. inclusive to stream running from C.12.a.5.3. into River STEENBECK at C.11.a.9.0. exclusive.

d. BARRAGE.
   Zero to Zero plus 4 minutes barrage will be on present line of enemy posts. Heavies will shoot in vicinity of MONT DU HIBOU.
   At zero plus 4 barrage will lift 100 yards. At zero plus 8 barrage will lift another 100 yards-where it will remain as a box barrage for 20 minutes. At that time it will slow down but will continue on same line for half an hour.

e. FORMATION. Companies will advance under barrage in two waves, first wave with moppers-up keeping close under barrage and second wave establishing posts as under :-

   "A" Coy.   "C" Coy.
   C.5.d.4.2.   Farm C.11.b.9.6.
   C.11.b.7.8.   C.12.a.0.3.
                           C.12.a.1.1.

   Each post will be garrisoned by 2 sections. On posts being established, remainder of Companies will withdraw to former support positions East and West of STEENBECK.

f. POSITION OF ASSEMBLY.
   At zero Companies will be in position, first wave on East bank of STEENBECK, second wave on West bank close to Bridgeheads.

g. Zero will be notified later - very probably 1 a.m. 13/8/17.

h. ACKNOWLEDGE.

11/8/17.   F.H.Rynman Lieut. & Adjt.

1/6th Bn. Gloucestershire Regt.

Battalion Operation Order No. 25.   17th August, 1917.

Ref. Sheet 28 N.W.

1. **MOVE.**   The Battalion will move into Support position in O.G.1 area tonight.
   Starting point : Bridge 2A.   Route : Bridge 2A and trench board track. Order of march : Hdqrs. "D" "B" "C" "A"
   Headquarters will pass Starting point at 8 pm., remainder of Battalion following at 100 yards distance between platoons.

2. **GUIDES.**   Guides provided by 1/8th Bn. Worcester Regt. will be at junction of Trench Board track with O.G.1 at 9 pm. to lead "D" & "B" Coys. to their positions. Guides from "A" & "C" Coys. will reconnoitre positions and meet their respective Companies under Company arrangements.

3. **TRANSPORT.**   One limber per Company will report to Coy. Hdqrs. at 7-15 pm. Lewis Guns, dixies and mess stores will be loaded immediately and limbers will proceed independently and off-load at junction of trench board track with ADMIRALS Road where Companies will pick up loads Coys. will detail representatives to accompany limbers.

4. **BATTALION HEADQUARTERS.**
                     Battalion Headquarters will move to CIVILISATION FARM.

5.   "All in" reports will be rendered in the usual manner. Sketch maps showing Coy. dispositions will also be rendered as soon as possible.

17/8/17.   [signature]   Lieut. & Adjt.

   NOTE:-   "D" & "B" Coys. will be taking over from "C" & "D" Companies, 1/8th Bn. Worcester Regt. respectively.

1/6th Bn. Gloucestershire Regiment.

Battalion Operation Order No.26.   18th August, 1917.

═══

Ref. Sheet 28 N.W.

1. **RELIEF.**   "B" & "D" Companies will be relieved by the 1/8th Bn. Worcester Regiment tonight.

2. **GUIDES.**   "B" & "D" Companies will each provide 1 guide per platoon and 1 for Company Hdqrs. to be at junction of Trench Board Track with C.G.1 (near old Battalion Headquarters) at 8 pm.

3. **TRANSPORT.**   1 limber each for "D" & "B" Coys. will be at today's ration dump (where Trench Board track crosses ADMIRA'S Road) at 9 pm, to take out Lewis Guns, Coy. rations and mess stores. Representatives to accompany limbers.

4. **DESTINATION.**   After relief, "B" & "D" Coys. will proceed to CANAL BANK.

5. **BATTALION HEADQUARTERS.**
    Battalion Headquarters will move to CANAL BANK on completion of relief. Capt.R.G.TITLEY, M.C. will assume command of "A" & "C" Companies and will take over present Battalion Headquarters.

18/8/17.   [signature] Lieut. &Adjt.,

1/6th Bn. Gloucestershire Regiment.

Battalion Operation Order No. 22.   20th August, 1917.

Ref. Sheet 28 N.W.

1. **RELIEF.** The Battalion will relieve the 1/8th Bn. Worcester Regiment in the line tonight.

2. **DISPOSITIONS.**
   "B" Coy. 1 plat. "C" Coy. will relieve "B" Coy. 1/8th Bn. Worc Regt.
   "D" Coy. will relieve "A" Coy. 1/8th Bn. Worc. Regt.
   "C" Coy. less 1 plat. att. "B" Coy. will relieve parts of Worc. Coys. in ALBERTA.
   "A" Coy. will remain in present position.

3. **ORDER OF MARCH.**
   Hdqrs. "B" att. plat. "D" Coy.
   Headquarters will move off from Bridge 2A at 8 pm.
   "B" Coy. 8-15 pm. "D" Coy. 8-30 pm. Distance between platoons : 200 yards. "C" Coy. less 1 platoon will fall in at O.G.1. behind "D" Coy.

4. **TRANSPORT.** Two limbers for "B" "D" & Hdqrs. will be at Ambulance ration dump at 6-30 pm to carry Lewis Guns and mess stores. Limbers will proceed in advance and dump loads at junction of Trench Board track with ADMIRALS Road. Representatives will accompany limbers.

Lieut. & Adjt.

20/8/17.

1/6th Bn. Gloucestershire Regiment.

Battalion Operation Order No. 38.   22nd August, 1917.

Ref. Sheet 28 N.W.

1. In conjunction with troops on our Right and Left the Battalion will attack and capture the line WINNIPEG - POELCAPELLE Road from SPRINGFIELD exclusive to road junction C.6.central where a post will be established to connect with 33rd Infantry Brigade who will also have a post at cross roads C.6.b.1.4.

2. The attack will be made by tanks supported by Infantry who will, after capture of line, consolidate and hold it.
    On the Brigade front, tanks will take VANCOUVER which will be included in our line. If tanks do not arrive no Infantry attack will be made on VANCOUVER, but wave, moving behind creeping barrage will occupy and hold any advantageous positions they may discover.
    Should enemy evacuate VANCOUVER owing to barrage, it will be occupied at once.

3. The attack will be carried out by "B" & "D" Companies in accordance with orders already issued.

4. Zero for Tanks will be 4-45 am.

5. BARRAGE.
    An Artillery barrage will open at Zero plus 10 minutes, starting 200 yards East of Road KEERSELARE - ST. JULIEN, and creeping forward at the rate of 100 yards in 8 minutes.
    From Zero plus 1 hour 6 minutes to Zero plus 3 hours 6 minutes, barrage will fire on LANGEMARCK LINE.
    At Zero plus 3 hours 6 minutes barrage ceases.

6. A Smoke Barrage will also be put down on our Left.

7. CONTACT AEROPLANE.
    Contact Aeroplane will fly over objectives at Zero plus 1 hour and at Zero plus 2 hours, at which times Infantry will light red flares whether called on or not.
    At other times, flares will only be lit when called for by the aeroplane.

9-30 pm.
21/8/17.   Lieut. & Adjt.

1/6th Bn. Gloucestershire Regiment.

Appendix to Battalion Operation Order No.28.   21st August, 1917.

Ref. Map POELCAPELLE

1.   The Battalion will attack line C.6.c.8.7. – VANCOUVER – SPRINGFIELD exclusive on the morning of 22nd instant, in conjunction with Tanks.
   Right Boundary of Battalion : HILLOCK FARM inclusive – SPRINGFIELD exclusive.

   Left Boundary of Battalion : MON DU HIBOU inclusive – road junction C.6.c.8.7. inclusive.

   "D" Company will attack on the Right.
   "B" Coy. will attack on the Left.
   "D" Company will follow up behind barrage keeping touch with 1/7th Warwickshire Regt. on their Right and will establish post at Dugouts N.W. of SPRINGFIELD and cross roads at C.6.d.3.3.

   "B" Company will occupy VANCOUVER Farm and will establish a post at C.6.central to connect with 53rd Brigade on the Left.

   2 platoons of "C" Company will be in support at MON DU HIBOU and 2 platoons of "C" Coy. at C.11.b.3.5.
   "A" Company will be in reserve at ALBERTA.

2.   Barrage Table will be issued to Companies.

3.   Battalion Headquarters and Regimental Aid post will be at ALBERTA.

4.   Forward Battalion Headquarters will be at MON DU HIBOU.

5.   ACKNOWLEDGE.

21/8/17.   *[signature]*   Lieut. & Adjt.

            Copies : All Coys.
                    1/7th R.Warwickshire Rgt.
                    8th Lincolns.
                    145th Inf. Bde.
                    War diary.

1/6th Bn. Gloucestershire Regiment.

Battalion Operation Order No.29.   23rd August, 1917.

Ref. Sheet 28 N.W.

1. RELIEF.   The Battalion will be relieved by the 1/4th Bn. Gloucestershire Regt. tonight and will proceed to dug-outs in Canal Bank.

2. GUIDES.   "B" "C" & "D" Companies will provide 1 guide per platoon and 1 for each Company Hdqrs. to be at Battalion Hdqrs., ALBERTA at 10-45 pm. Post guides will be provided by Companies at Company Hdqrs. under orders by O's C. Coys. concerned.

3. DISPOSITIONS.   The 1/4th Glouc. Regt. will take over as under :-
    "D" Coy. 4th Glouc. from "B" Coy. in Left Front Sector.
    "C" Coy.   -do-   "D" Coy. in Right Front Sector.
    "B" Coy.   -do-   2 plat. "A" Coy. at ALBERTA.
    "A" Coy.   -do-   2 plat. "A" Coy. in O.G.1.

4. ROUTE FROM TRENCHES.
    Trench Board track to Bridge 2A.

5. BILLETING PARTY.
    Billeting party has gone on and will meet Companies at Bridge 2A.

6.   O's C. "B" "C" & "D" Coys. will report personally at Battalion Headquarters when their reliefs are complete.

7.   Any post, the relief of which is not complete by daylight will remain until relieved tomorrow night.

23/8/17.   [signature] Lieut. & Adjt.

1/6th Bn. Gloucestershire Regiment.

Battalion Operation Order No.30.   24th August, 1917.

Ref. Sheet 28 N.W.

1. **MOVE.** The Battalion will move to KRUGERSBERG Camp this morning.

2. **MARCH.** The Battalion will move off in the order "A" "B" "C" "D"
   Leading platoon of "A" Company will move off at 9-30 am.
   Distance between platoons ; 200 yards.

3. **BILLETING PARTY.**
   1 N.C.O. per Company will report to Lieut. F.H.Coombs at Battalion Headquarters, Canal Bank at 8 am.

4. **STORES.** Limbers for Lewis Guns and Mess Stores will be at Ambulance Ration Dump at 9 am.

F.S.Reynman Lieut. & Adjt.

23/8/17.

1/6th Bn. Gloucestershire Regiment.

Battalion Operation Order No.31.   28th August, 1917.

1. **MOVE.** The Battalion will move tomorrow to SCHOOL CAMP, ST. JAN TEN BIEZEN, entraining at VLAMERTINGHE.

2. **PARADE.** Companies will parade ready to move at 9-40 am. Battalion will move off in rear of 7th Worcesters, 200 yards distance between Companies. Order of march :-

    Hdqrs. "A" "B" "C" "D"

3. **ADVANCE PARTY.** Advance party of 1 N.C.O. per Coy. and 1 each from Transport and Q.M. Branch will report to Lieut. W.H. Coombs at Battalion Headquarters at 8-30 am. This party will proceed on bicycles. Transport and Q.M. providing their own mounts.

4. **TRANSPORT.** Valises and mess stores will be on track behind Hdqrs. Mess at 8-30 am. Pioneers will load.

5. Sick parade 7 am. Medical Officer will select 40 men for accommodation on lorries which will be at Marsh Farm at 10 am.

F.T. Wyman, Lieut. & Adjt.

28/8/17.

Vol 30

30 R
8 sheets

Experimental

War Diary
of
1/6th Bn. The Gloucestershire Regiment, T.F.

From 1/9/14 to 30/9/14

(vol. XXX)

Army Form C. 2118.

WAR DIARY
or
INTELLIGENCE SUMMARY

(Erase heading not required.)

1/6th Bn. Gloucestershire Regt.
September 1917.

Place	Date	Hour	Summary of Events and Information	Remarks and references to Appendices
St JAN TER BIEZEN.	Sept. 1		At School Camp	
Do.	2		Do.	
Do.	3		Do.	
Do.	4		Do.	
Do.	5		Do.	
Do.	6		Do.	
Do.	7		Do.	
Do.	8		Do.	
Do.	9		Do.	
Do.	10		Do.	
Do.	11		Do.	
Do.	12		Do.	
Do.	13		Do.	
Do.	14		Do.	
Do.	15		Do.	
Do.	16		Do. Portion of Batt. moved by road to ZUTKERQUE.	Order 16.9.17 to T.O. WINNEZEELE SA
	17		Batt moved from School Camp to ZUTKERQUE. Entrained at ABEELE & detrained at AUDRUIQ.	B.O.O. No.32 By WINNEZEELE SA
ZUTKERQUE	18		Remainder of Transport entrained at HOPOUTRE and detrained at AUDRUIQ. Trains delayed. Batt arrived AUDRUIQ at 10.25 A.M. Transport all in by 4 p.m.	B.O.18.9.17.
Do.	19		Brigade Scheme 'B' at NORDAUSQUE	
Do.	20		Battalion Area	
Do.	21		Divisional Scheme at TOURNEHEM.	Bne 20.9.17
Do.	22		Battalion Area	

Army Form C. 2118.

WAR DIARY (6m²)
or
INTELLIGENCE SUMMARY

(Erase heading not required.)

1/6th Bn. Gloucestershire Regt.
September 1919.

Instructions regarding War Diaries and Intelligence Summaries are contained in F. S. Regs., Part II. and the Staff Manual respectively. Title Pages will be prepared in manuscript.

Place	Date	Hour	Summary of Events and Information	Remarks and references to Appendices
	1919			
ZUTKERQUE	Sept 23		Battalion Area	
Do	24		Firing (Field) on GUEMP. Range.	B.R.O. 23.9.19
Do	25		A Coy (Bde Field Firing Coy) also Coys Classification range at NORTBECOURT.	B.R.O. 24.9.19
Do	26		Battalion Area	
Do	27		Brigade Scheme at NORDAUSQUE	O.O. No 33 dd 27 Sept.
Do	28		Battalion Area	20.00
Do	29		Part of Transport moved to DRAKE CAMP. Training in Northern Area	B.O. 28.9.19 by 2 SNW
Do	30		Voluntary Church Service	B.O 27.9.19

Casualties during the month of September
Officers —
O.R. — 2

Accidentally wounded — 33

Disappeared during the month —

Ration Strength 30-9-19 24 802

A.H. Mehuer by Lt. Col.
Commdg. 1/6 Gloucestershire Regt.

2449 Wt. W14957/M90 750,000 1/16 J.B.C. & A. Forms/C.2118/12.

1/6th Bn. Gloucestershire Regiment.

Battalion Operation Order No.32.   16th September, 1917.

Ref. Sheet HAZEBROUCK 5A, 1/100,000.

1. **MOVE.** The Battalion will move to ZUTKERQUE tomorrow 17th instant. The Battalion will entrain at ABEELE and detrain at AUDRUICQ.

2. **PARADE.** The Battalion will parade in mass on Brigade Parade Ground at 2-30 pm. Markers will report on Ground at 2-20 pm. Interval of 200 yards between Companies will be maintained on the march.

3. **LEWIS GUNS.** Lewis Guns will be loaded on the limbers at the Transport Lines by 10 am. One Lewis Gunner per Company will report to Transport Serjeant at 2-30 pm, to accompany limbers.

4. **OFFICERS' VALISES AND MESS STORES.**
   Valises and all mess stores will be at entrance to Camp at 9-15 am. These will be loaded on a lorry provided for the purpose, by the pioneers.
   6 pioneers will be detailed to proceed with lorry to unload at ABEELE and load contents on the train. On arrival at AUDRUICQ a lorry will meet the train and convey valises and stores to billets.
   1 representative from the Q.M.Stores, Headquarters Mess and each Company Mess will report to R.Q.M.S. Gregory at AUDRUICQ Station. This party will load the lorry and proceed in it to billets.

5. **TRANSPORT.** Transport will proceed in two trains and entrain at HOPOUTRE at 4 pm & 8 pm. respectively. First train (4pm) will take cookers, mess cart, water carts, maltese cart, riding horses and bicycles. Second train (8pm) will take all remaining transport.

6. **LOADING OF TRANSPORT.**
   O's C. Companies will each detail 1 N.C.O. and 24 men to report, on training ground near Headquarters Mess, to an Officer to be detailed by O.C. "B" Company. Parade in marching order at 2 pm. party will proceed to HOPOUTRE Station to load Brigade Transport and will report to Brigade Transport Officer by 4 pm. This party will travel to AUDRUICQ on the second transport train (8pm). The 7th Worcesters are finding the unloading party at AUDRUICQ.
   Second Lieut.W.C.TOWNSEND will proceed to AUDRUICQ on the first transport train (4 pm).

7. **DRUMS.** The following men will collect the side drums and big drum from the Q.M.Stores at 11 am tomorrow.
   No.265275 Pte.W.Denley   H.Q.
   No.266785 Pte.E.Poole   "B"
   No.267445 Pte.E.Jones   "C"
   No.249112 Pte.M.Merriman   "C"
   No.-31447 Pte.G.Richardson   "D"
   No.265281 Pte.W.Thomas   "D"
   No.265029 Pte.H.Benstead   "D"
   No.265485 Pte.W.Healey   "D"
   O.C. "D" Company will detail 1 Serjeant to take charge of party, which will parade at 2-30 pm in rear of "A" Coy. This party is responsible for the drums until arrival at billets in ZUTKERQUE.

Battalion Operation Order No.32 (Contd).

8. CAMP. The Camp is to be left xxxxxxx scrupulously clean. The final inspection of Camp will be held at 1-45 pm.

9. COOKERS. Transport for cookers will be at Camp at 1-30 pm. Dinners will please be arranged accordingly.

BATTALION ORDERS.

1. Orderly Officer for tomorrow - 2/Lieut.W.R.VOWLES.
2. Sick parade 8-30 am. Orderly Room 10-30 am.

15/9/17.

Lieut. & A/Adjt.

1/6th Bn. Gloucestershire Regt.

Battalion Operation Order No.33.   27th September, 1917.

===

Ref. Training Map, 1/20,000.

1.   The 144 Brigade will attack on the whole
    Divisional Front -
        7th WORCESTERS on the Right.
        6th GLOUCESTERS in the Centre.
        4th GLOUCESTERS on the Left.

2.   BATTALION FRONTAGE :-

        Right Boundary - track running from J.26.d.8.7.
        through WELLINGTON inclusive to INCH HOUSE exclusive.

        Left Boundary - track running from J.27.b.2.1. through
        QUEBEC FARM (exclusive) to OXFORD HOUSE (exclusive).

3.   OBJECTIVES :-
        1st Objective - Blue Line J.33.a.5.2. to J.33.b.8.8.
                        including strong points YORK FARM
                        and WINCHESTER FARM.

        2nd Objective - Red Line from J.33.d.5.2. to J.34.c.4.7.
                        including strong point STOKE FARM
                        and WELLINGTON.

        3rd Objective - Pink Line from P.4.a.2.4. to J.34.d.0.2.
                        including strong point VACHER FARM.

4.   In conjunction with the 4th GLOUCESTERS and the
    7th WORCESTERS
        "A" Coy. will attack & consolidate 1st objective.
        "B" Coy.   "   "   "   "   2nd   "
        "C" Coy.   "   "   "   "   3rd   "
        "D" Coy. Battalion Reserve.

5.   ARTILLERY BARRAGE as per table attached.

6.   BATTALION HEADQUARTERS and First Aid Post on road at
    J.27.a.5.2.

7.   ZERO - 10-30 am.

                                        Lieut. & A/Adjt.
27/9/17.

        Copy 1   retained.
              2-5 Companies.
              6   4th Gloucesters.
              7   7th Worcesters.
              8   144 Infantry Brigade.
              9   M.G.Coy.

ARTILLERY BARRAGE.

Artillery Barrage will move at the rate of 50 yards in 2 minutes to Green line where it will dwell for 30 minutes, moving on at Zero plus 50 minutes. It will then similarly move at the rate of 50 yards in 2 minutes to Red line where it will dwell for 30 minutes.

1/6th Battalion Gloucestershire Regiment.

Battalion Operation Order No. 34.   30th September, 1917.

Ref. HAZEBROUCK Sheet 5A.
POELCAPPELLE - Edition 3. 1/10,000
Sheet 28 N.W. 1/20,000

1. **MOVE.** The Battalion, less Transport which proceeded by road on the 29th instant, will proceed to the forward area tomorrow, 1st October.
    Entraining Station for the whole of personnel and remainder of Transport : AUDRUICQ.
    Detraining Station for Battalion personnel : VLAMERTINGHE.
    Detraining Station for Transport : PESELHOEK.
    Destination : Hdqrs. "A" "B" & "D" Coys. - BRAKE CAMP.
    -do-   : "C" Company - REIGERSBURG CAMP.

2. **PARADES.** "C" Company will parade in marching order outside Battalion Headquarters at 3-40 am and will march to AUDRUICQ Station, where they will entrain at 5 am.
    Headquarters, "A" "B" & "D" Companies will parade in marching order outside Battalion Headquarters at 7-50 am. Formation : column of route (facing the Church). Head of column to be opposite Battalion Guard. Order of march :-
    Headquarters "A" "B" "D"
    The Battalion (less "C" Coy.) will march to AUDRUICQ Station and entrain at 9 am.

3. **WORKING PARTY.** On arrival of "C" Company at VLAMERTINGHE, they will march (with 3 other Companies from the Brigade) to REIGERSBURG Camp, direct. "C" Company made up to 100 diggers, will be required to go up on the evening of the 1st October to continue the buried cable from SPOT FARM to ARBRE. Work to commence at 8-30 pm. Arrangements for tools and also the rendezvous, are being made by O.C. 48th Divisional Signals.

4. **TRANSPORT.** Transport for "C" Coy. cooker and Lewis Gun limber will report to "C" Company Hdqrs. at 4-30 am tomorrow, 1st October. These will proceed to AUDRUICQ Station where they will entrain at 6 am. The Company cooks and 2 Lewis Gunners will accompany cooker and limber.
    Detraining Station : PESELHOEK.
    Destination : REIGERSBURG CAMP.

    The remainder of transport, namely :- Riders 6, pack 7, Lewis Gun limbers and horses (less "C" Coy's), tool limbers and horses, water carts and horses, bomb limbers and horses, cookers and horses (less "C" Coy's), mess cart and horse, and maltese cart and horse, will entrain at AUDRUICQ at 12 noon. Transport for Company cookers and Lewis Gun limbers will report to respective Company Hdqrs. at 10-30 am.
    Detraining Station : PESELHOEK.
    Destination : BRAKE CAMP.
    T.O. will arrange.

5. **OFFICERS' VALISES & MESS STORES.** The Mess Cart will report to "C" Company Hdqrs. tonight at 9 pm. Valises and mess stores of "C" Company will be loaded and mess cart will proceed to AUDRUICQ Station.

(1)

(2)

OFFICERS' VALISES & MESS STORES (Contd).
O.C. "C" Company will detail 2 men to go with Mess Cart and act as guard over the valises and mess stores.

Valises and mess stores of Headquarters, "A" "B" & "D" Companies will be dumped near the road on Headquarters Football Field, at 7 am. These will be loaded by the pioneers on a lorry provided for the purpose.

The pioneers will be detailed to proceed with the lorry and will unload contents at AUDRUICQ and load same on the train.

BATTALION ORDERS.

1. **BATTLE STRENGTH.**
O.C. Companies and Officer i/c Headquarters Details will render a battle strength to Battalion Hdqrs., immediately on arrival in the forward area. The battle strength of platoons must be shewn separately and details given of other ranks who are to be left out of action. This return will accompany the "All in" Report.

2. **CASUALTY REPORT.**
A Daily Casualty Report will be rendered to Battalion Headquarters by 3 pm daily as from October 1st until further notice.

3. **MACHINE GUN COMPANY.**
On arrival in new area, O.C. Companies will each detail 2 other ranks to report immediately to Battalion Headquarters in marching order. These men will be attached to the 144 Machine Gun Company.

4.   Orderly Officer for tomorrow — 2/Lieut.C.L.MORRIS
    Orderly Officer next for duty — 2/Lieut.C.C.BUTLER.

Lieut. & A/Adjt.,

30/9/17.   for O.C. 1/6th Bn. Gloucestershire Regt.

X: O/C C Coy.

Please render your Battle Strength tonight.

Confidential

Vol 31

1/6th Gloucestershire Regiment

WAR DIARY

1st October – 31st October 1917

VOLUME XXXI

E.W.

31.R.
25 what

Army Form C. 2118.

WAR DIARY
or
INTELLIGENCE SUMMARY
(Erase heading not required.)

Instructions regarding War Diaries and Intelligence Summaries are contained in F.S. Regs., Part II. and the Staff Manual respectively. Title Pages will be prepared in manuscript.

Place	Date	Hour	Summary of Events and Information	Remarks and references to Appendices
ZUTKERQUE	1917 1st Oct.		Battn. (less Transport which moved by Road) moved by Rail to BRAKE CAMP. Entraining Station AUDRICQ. Detraining Station VLAMERTINGHE. "C" Company encamped at REIGERSBURG CAMP. "C" Company working party same evening Buried Cable - SPOT FARM - ARBRE.	HAZEBROUCK Sheet 5a POELCAPELLE E4.3 SHEET 28 NW Br. OO 34.
VLAMERTINGHE	2		"C" Coy Continue work on Cable as on 1st.	28 NW
BRAKE CAMP				
do.	3		do	28 NW
do.	4		do	28 NW Br. OO 34a " OO 34b.
CANAL BANK	5		Battn. moved to CANAL BANK 2.15pm VIA CHEMIN MILITAIRE - SALVATION CORNER.	28 NW Br. OO 35. " OO 35 a.
DAMBRE CAMP	6		Battn. moved to DAMBRE CAMP in the morning.	POELCAPELLE 28 NW
do.	7		In Camp.	
IRISH FM.	7		Battn. moved to IRISH FARM 8.30 a.m. Heavy rain a/noon and evening.	28 N.W. Br. OO 35. " OO 35 a.
DAMBRE CAMP	8		Battn. moved back to DAMBRE CAMP 4.30 p.m.	28 NW
TRENCHES.	9		Battn. moved to Front line and relieved 1/1 BUCKS. Proceeded by tow via WIELTJE - St JEAN and thence by foot ADMIRALS ROAD and Trench Board track. Battn. attacked - 5.30 a.m. See Appendix attached.	Br. OO 36. 18 N OO 37
TRENCHES	10		Battn. relieved by 26 Brigade 4 Seaforths Right Front, 5 Camerons Left Front. Returned to SIEGE CAMP via temporary shelter at IRISH FARM.	POELCAPELLE 28 NW Br. OO 37a.
SIEGE CAMP	11			

Army Form C. 2118.

WAR DIARY
or
INTELLIGENCE SUMMARY

(Erase heading not required.)

Instructions regarding War Diaries and Intelligence Summaries are contained in F.S. Regs., Part II. and the Staff Manual respectively. Title Pages will be prepared in manuscript.

Place	Date 1917	Hour	Summary of Events and Information	Remarks and references to Appendices
SIEGE CAMP	12		Battn. moved 3.15pm to SCHOOL CAMP at ST JAN TER BIEZEN. Joined at Camp by Dump party from HOUTKERQUE. hours/officers 2/Lieuts McKenna, Morgan, Harper and Cohen.	SHEET 27.28 1/40,000
ST JAN TER BIEZEN	13		Battn. moved to TINQUES (1st ARMY AREA) 8.45am by Rail. Entraining Station HOPOUTRE Detraining station LIGNY ST FLOCHEL	Bn. 0.0.38 HAZEBROUCK 5a 1/100,000.
TINQUES	14		Arrived 2.30pm	Bn. 0.0.39
TINQUES	15		Battn. moved to VILLERS AU BOIS by Road via FERMONT and ACQ.	LENS 11. Bn. 0.0.40
VILLERS AU BOIS	16		In Camp.	
do	17		Battn. moved forward and relieved 28th CANADIAN BATT. in Support. (LA CHAUDIÈRE) MARQUEIL and	36c S.W.
VIMY	18		In Support.	Bn. 0.0.41.
do	19		In Support.	
do	20		In Support.	Sheet.
do	21		Battn. moved forward and took over Front Line from 1/8 WORCESTERS and 1/4 GLOUCE STERSHIRES	36c S.W.
FRONT LINE	22		In the Front Line	Bn. 0.0.41a
do	23		do	Sheet
do	24		do	36c S.W.

Army Form C. 2118.

WAR DIARY
or
INTELLIGENCE SUMMARY

(Erase heading not required.)

Instructions regarding War Diaries and Intelligence Summaries are contained in F. S. Regs., Part II. and the Staff Manual respectively. Title Pages will be prepared in manuscript.

Place	Date 1917 Oct	Hour	Summary of Events and Information	Remarks and references to Appendices
TRENCHES	26		Battn. relieved by 1/7 Battn. WORCESTERSHIRES. and proceeded to CELLAR CAMP at NEUVILLE St VAAST in Brigade Reserve	Sheet LENS 11. Bn OO.42
NEUVILLE St.	27		CELLAR CAMP.	LENS 11
VAAST	28		do	
do	29		do	
do	30		do	
do	31		do.	

Casualties during the month of October 1917.

	Officers	O.Rs
Killed	1	52
Died (wounds)	1	4
Wounded	4	153
Wounded (missing)		3
Missing		39
	5	79
Drafts received during the month		
Ration Strength. 31.4.17	28	633

2449 Wt. W14957/M90 750,000 1/16 J.B.C. & A. Forms/C.2118/12.

OPERATION ORDERS No. 348
by
LT.Col.H.St.G.Schomberg, Comdg. 1/6th Bn.Gloucestershire Regt.

===

Ref. Sheet 28 N.W.

1. **MOVE.**   The Battalion will move to Canal Bank
   this afternoon.   Route : Chemin Militaire - Salvation
   Corner - Bridge 3A.

2. **PARADE.**   The Battalion will move off in the order

         "A" "B" "C" "D" "HQ"

   Leading platoon of "A" Company will move off at 1-45 pm.
   Distance between platoons : 100 yards.

3. **LEWIS GUNS, MESS STORES, ETC.**
   Limbers for Lewis Guns and mess stores
   will be at the Camp at 1-45 pm.   1 Lewis Gunner & 1
   servant per Company will accompany limbers.   Stores
   will be dumped at Bridge 3A.

4. **ADVANCE PARTY.**
   Lieut.W.J.H.POPE & 1 other rank from
   Headquarters have proceeded to the Canal Bank in
   advance, and will allot dug-outs for the Battalion.

                                                   Lieut. & A/Adjt.,

4/10/17.   for O.C. 1/6th Bn. Gloucestershire Rgt.

        Copies :-
           1 - 4 Companies.
              5 Transport Officer
              6 Quartermaster.
         7 & 8 War Diary.

OPERATION ORDERS No. 34b
by
Lt.Col.H.St.G.Schomberg, Comdg. 1/6th Bn.Gloucestershire Regt.

Ref. Sheet 20 N.W.

1. <u>MOVE.</u> Unless the Battalion is ordered forward during the night, the Battalion will move to DAMBRE Camp, tomorrow morning the 5th instant.

2. <u>PARADE.</u> Head of "C" Coy. will cross Bridge 3A at 9 am. Order of march :-

    "C" "B" "A" "D" "H.Q."

    100 yards interval will be maintained between platoons.
    Route : Bridge 3A - Salvation Corner - Chemin Militaire.

3. <u>MESS STORES.</u> Loaded on limbers on road by Bridge 4 by 8-30 am.

4. <u>LEWIS GUNS.</u> Lewis Guns will be loaded on limbers by Bridge 3A as the platoons pass. 1 Lewis Gunner per Company will accompany limbers.

5. <u>BILLETING.</u> Lieut.W.H.COOMBS and a party to be detailed by him from the light duty men, will proceed to DAMBRE Camp, in advance.

6. <u>TRANSPORT.</u> Transport Officer will arrange transport for cookers and Q.M.Stores to join Battalion at DAMBRE Camp. (including packs & valises).

                                    Lieut. & A/Adjt.,
4/10/17.   for O.C. 1/6th Bn. Gloucestershire Regt.

            Copies :-
                1 - 4 Companies.
                    5 Transport Officer
                    6 Quartermaster
                    7 Lieut.W.H.Coombs.
                    8 Retained.

1/6th Bn. Gloucestershire Regiment.

Battalion Operation Order No. 35. 6th October, 1917.

Ref: Sheet 28 N.W.

1. **MOVE.** The Battalion will move to IRISH FARM (C.27.a.15) tomorrow morning, 7th instant.

2. **PARADE.** Head of column will leave the entrance to the Camp at 8-30 am. Order of march :-
"Hdqrs" "A" "B" "C" "D"
Dress : fighting order. Route : Chemin Militaire - Bridge 2A - Trench board track to Irish Farm. Distance between platoons : 100 yards.

3. **WORKING PARTY TO DRAW BIVOUAC SHEETS.** Lieut. C.C. BUTLER and 20 other ranks to be detailed by O.C. "B" Company will report to Lieut. HUMPHRIES at Red Heart, CANAL BANK at 9 am, tomorrow 7th instant, to draw bivouac sheets. This party will parade at 7-30 am. Dress : fighting order.

4. **GUIDES.** One N.C.O. per Company and 1 N.C.O. from Battalion Hdqrs. will report to the Adjutant's tent at 7-30 am tomorrow. These N.C.O's will proceed to IRISH FARM in advance, ascertain the site of Camp, and return to SALVATION CORNER, where they will meet the Battalion.

5. **LEWIS GUNS.** Lewis Guns will be loaded at 8 am. Additional Lewis Gun drums as required by Companies, should be drawn from the Transport and loaded, at the same time.

6. **MESS STORES.** Mess Stores will be loaded on Lewis Gun limbers at 8 am.

7. **DIXIES.** Dixies to cook tea at IRISH FARM will be loaded on Lewis Gun limbers at 8 am. The cookers will remain behind to cook meat for the 9th instant. 2 cooks per Coy. will proceed to IRISH FARM, and 2 will remain with the cookers.

8. **PACKS.** O's C. Companies and Officer i/c Headquarters Details will arrange for packs to be stored in one tent in the respective lines. Company storemen and 1 other rank from Headquarters will guard packs until transport arrives to convey them to the Q.M. Stores. Packs to be in by 7-30 am.

9. **OFFICERS' VALISES & SURPLUS MESS STORES** to be dumped in same tents as packs at 7-45 am.

10. **RATIONS.** Rations for the 7th instant will be carried on the man. Transport Officer will arrange for 2 limbers to be at the Camp at 8 am. Rations for the 8th instant will be loaded on these limbers at 8 am.

11. **WATER.** All waterbottles must be filled before the Battalion moves. Q.M. & T.O. will arrange for 100 petrol tins and 50 spare waterbottles (all filled) to be brought to IRISH FARM in the early afternoon of the 7th inst.

12. **SHOVELS.** 20 shovels will be loaded on each Lewis Gun limber at 8 am. Q.M. will arrange. ~~Tommy cookers, Improvised Trench Food Heaters, Rum and Whale Oil~~

13. **IMPROVISED TRENCH FOOD HEATERS, RUM & WHALE OIL,** *Tommy cookers*. The Quartermaster will meet Coy. Q.M. Sergts. in the Camp at 8 am to distribute the above, which will be conveyed to IRISH FARM on the ration limbers.

(1)

(2)

14. **FIGHTING EQUIPMENT.**

Lieut. C.C. BUTLER, 1 Sergeant (with a knowledge of bombing) & 2 other ranks to be detailed by O.C. "A" Company, will draw fighting equipment tomorrow at 2 pm. Place : CANAL BANK, I.2.a.1.9. Lieut. C.C. BUTLER will report to Adjutant's Tent at 7-20 am tomorrow for instructions. The N.C.O. & 2 other ranks from "A" Company will report to Battalion Headquarters at IRISH FARM at 12-30 pm tomorrow.

15. **SUMMER TIME.**

Summer time will cease on the night 6/7th October, at 1 am on the 7th October. Watches will be put back to 12 midnight.

16. Sick parade 7 am.

Lieut. & A/Adjt.,
6/10/17.   for O.C. 1/6th Bn. Gloucestershire Rgt.

  Copies 1 Retained
      2 & 3 War Diary.
      4 Off. i/c H.Q. Details.
      5 - 8 Companies.
      9 Transport Officer.
      10 Quartermaster.

OPERATION ORDERS   No.35a
by
Lt.Col.H.St.G.Schomberg, Comdg. 1/6th Bn.Gloucestershire Regt.

==

Ref. Sheet 28 N.W.

1. **MOVE.**   The Battalion will move back to DAMBRE Camp this afternoon.

2. **PARADE.**   The Battalion will parade at 4-30 pm., and will move off in the order -

    "H.Q." "A" "B" "C" "D"

    100 yards interval will be maintained between platoons.
    Route : Bridge 2A - Salvation Corner - Dambre Camp.

3. **LEWIS GUNS, MESS STORES, ETC.**
    Limbers for Lewis Guns and mess stores will be at Irish Farm at 4 pm. 1 Lewis Gunner & 1 servant per Company will accompany limbers.

4. **ACCOMMODATION.**
    Companies will take over the same accommodation at Dambre Camp as before.

5. **TRANSPORT.**
    Transport Officer will arrange transport to convey packs, valises & cookers to Dambre Camp.

                                    L.Neone
                                    Lieut. & A/Adjt.,
7/10/17.   for O.C. 1/6th Bn.Gloucestershire Regt.

OPERATION ORDERS NO.28.
by
Lt.Col.H.St.G.Schomberg, Comdg. 1/5th Bn.Gloucestershire Regt.

Ref. Sheet 28 N.W. - 1/20,000
POELCAPPELLE Sheet - 1/10,000

1. **RELIEF.** The Battalion will relieve the 146th Infantry Brigade in the front line tonight.

2. **DISPOSITIONS.** Companies will hold the line as follows :-
   - "A" Coy. - Right Front.
   - "B" Coy. - Left Front
   - "C" Coy. - Right Support
   - "D" Coy. - Left Support

3. **ADVANCE PARTY.** An Advance Party consisting of Capt. D.H.MARTON, M.C., 3 other Officers, and 8 other ranks have proceeded to the line in advance to lay tapes for front and support Companies to form up on.

4. **PARADE.** The Battalion will parade at 3-30 p.m. and will proceed by busses to AMIKALA ROAD. They will debus there and proceed to the line via Trench board track - Triangle - Alberta - Hubner Farm. 200 yards between platoons will be maintained.

5. **GUIDES.** Guides are arranged by the 146th Inf.Bde. 1 guide per platoon will meet the Battalion at HUBNER FM. 2/Lieut.C.W.LANGDON will proceed to HUBNER FARM in advance and superintend the guiding of the Battalion.

6. **LEWIS GUNS.** The Lewis Guns and the usual 24 drums per gun will be carried by the men and **not** loaded on the limbers. Spare Lewis Gun drums to be loaded on pack ponies immediately on receipt of these orders. These will be carried by the ponies to the TRIANGLE, where they will be picked up by Companies as they pass. *L.T.C bombs will be at TRIANGLE*

7. **MESS STORES FOR THE LINE** to be loaded on limber in Camp immediately. These should be limited to 3 sandbags per coy.

8. **RATIONS** for the 9th & 10th to be distributed to the men before the Battalion moves.

9. **WATER.** Waterbottles must be filled before the Batt. moves. Each Company will pick up 45 petrol tins filled with water at the TRIANGLE. Headquarters Details will pick up 40 tins. O.C. "D" Coy. will detail a party to convey 40 tins to Battalion H.Q. at WINCHESTER FARM. These 40 tins will form a small Battalion dump, and may be drawn on in case of emergency.

10. **SHOVELS** will be picked up by platoons where trench board track crosses Poelcappelle Road near Triangle. Each Company will take 28 shovels, Battalion H.Q. 12 shovels.

11. **KITS** may be placed on petrol tin limber and picked up by Companies at the Triangle.

12. **FIGHTING EQUIPMENT.** Flares, S.O.S. etc. will be drawn by Companies immediately on receipt of these orders. 2/Lieut.U.M.BEATTY will arrange and report complete.

(1)

13. **OFFICERS' VALISES & SURPLUS STORES** will be dumped in a hut as arranged by the Quartermaster, by 2-30 pm.

14. **WHALE OIL.** All ranks must rub their feet with whale oil.

[signature]

Lieut. & A/Adjt.

5/10/17.   for O.C. 1/6th Bn. Gloucestershire Regt.

Copies :- 1 & 2   War Diary.
          3 - 6   Companies
          7   Off. i/c H.Q. Details.
          8   Transport Officer.
          9   Quartermaster.

OPERATION ORDERS No.37.

by

Lt.Col.H.St.G.Schomberg, Comdg. 1/6th Bn.Gloucestershire Regt.

Ref. POELCAPPELLE Sheet – 1/10,000

1. **INFORMATION.** In conjunction with troops on the right and left, the 144th Infantry Brigade will attack tomorrow morning, 9th instant.

2. **FIRST OBJECTIVE.**
   Line running between OXFORD and SHAFT along gun pits in V.26.c. to just East of INCH HOUSE.

3. **SECOND OBJECTIVE.**
   Line running East of BERKS HOUSE to WALLEMOLEN, from about V.21.c.41. to D.4.a.46.

5. **ORDER OF ATTACK.**
   - 7th Worcesters – Right
   - 6th Gloucesters – Centre
   - 4th Gloucesters – Left
   - 8th Worcesters – Bde.Reserve.

6. **BATTALION FRONTAGE.**
   Left Boundary. Along N. boundary of Cemetery in V.26.d. to copse about V.26.c.81 exclusive to BERKS HOUSE exclusive.

   Right Boundary. Track running from D.2.b.01. to D.3.a.07, thence to MEBUS at V.27.d.18. exclusive.

7. Companies will attack in the following order :-
   - "A" & "B" Coy. – 1st Wave.
     - "A" Coy on the Right.
     - "B" Coy on the Left
   - "C" & "D" Coy. – 2nd Wave.
     - "C" Coy.on the Right
     - "D" Coy on the Left.

8. At Zero, "A" & "B" Companies will advance under barrage and capture 1st objective.

9. Dividing line between Companies - V.26.d.13. to N. end of gun pit about V.27.c.27.

10. **STRONG POINTS.**
    "A" Company will detail special parties to capture VACHER FARM and gun pits about D.2.b.67, and gun pit V.27.c.55.
    "B" Company will capture BURNS HOUSE and Cemetery in V.27.d.

11. **SECOND OBJECTIVE.**
    "C" & "D" Companies will move in close support of "A" & "B" Coys. up to 1st objective. At Zero plus 1 hour 46 minutes, will advance from 1st objective under barrage and capture 2nd objective.

12. **STRONG POINTS.**
    "C" Company will assist "A" Company if necessary in capturing gun pit about V.27.c.55 and will also assist 7th Worcesters in capturing MEBUS at V.27.d.18.
    "D" Company will assist 4th Gloucesters if necessary in the capture of BERKS HOUSE.

(2)

13. **BARRAGE TABLE.** At Zero, barrage will commence on line 150 yards in front of our present post. At Zero plus 4 barrage will move at the rate of 100 yards in 6 minutes, to 1st objective, where it will dwell for 1 hour & 10 minutes. At Zero plus 1 hour 46 minutes, barrage will move at the rate of 100 yards in 8 minutes.

14. Both objectives when gained will be consolidated, and line thinned out in depth. When final objective has been gained, a strong point will be constructed by "A" Company at V.27.c.84.

15. **CONTACT AEROPLANE.** Contact Aeroplane will fly over objectives at Zero plus 1 hour 30 minutes and at Zero plus 2 hours 30 minutes. Infantry will be ready to light red flares in lines, not groups, at these hours, but will not light flares unless called for by Klaxon Horn or dropping white lights.

An Aeroplane, the mission of which is to detect the approach of counter attacks, will be up continuously from Zero. When it observes hostile parties of 100 or more move into counter attack, it will drop a smoke bomb over that portion of the front to which enemy is moving.

This smoke bomb will burst about 100 feet below the aeroplane, into a white parachute flare which will descend slowly, leaving a long trail of brown smoke behind it.

16. 2 outpost Companies of the 145 Brigade will be holding the line at Zero, and remain there until the Battalion has passed through.

17. BATTALION HEADQUARTERS - WINCHESTER FARM.

18. 1st AID POST. - HUBNER FARM.

19. Dump of water, ammunition bombs etc. at Battalion Headquarters.

20. COMPLETION OF ASSEMBLY will be reported to Battalion Headquarters.

Lieut.Col.,

8/10/17. Comdg. 1/6th Bn. Gloucestershire Rgt.

Copies :-
1 & 2 War Diary
3 - 6 Companies.
    7 144 Inf. Bde.
    8 4th Gloucesters.
    9 7th Worcesters.

Ref. POELCAPPELLE MAP - 1/10,000

REPORT ON ATTACK BY 1/6th BN. GLOUCESTERSHIRE REGT.

ON MORNING OF 9th OCTOBER 1917.

1. The Battalion attacked as follows :-

   First Wave - "A" Company on the Right, "B" Company on the Left.

   Second Wave - "C" Company on the Right, "D" Company on the Left.

Both waves consisted of two lines each - two platoons of each Company being in each line.

Objectives.

   First Wave. - To capture first objective (from gun pit about V.27.c.63. to V.26.b.91.).

   Strong points - "B" Company to detail special parties to capture 2 MEBUS about V.26.d.46.and redoubt about V.26.d.55.70. "A" Company to detail special parties to capture VACHER HOUSE and gun pit about V.27.c.63.

   Second Wave - To capture second objective - V.27.a.49. to BERKS HOUSES exclusive.

   Strong points - "C" Company to detail special parties to assist 7th Worcesters in capture of MEBUS about V.27.d.10.60. "D" Company to detail special party to assist 4th Gloucesters in capture of BERKS HOUSES.

In the event of first wave being held up - second wave to fight their way through them and endeavour to keep up with barrage and reach second objective.

   Two parallel tapes were laid out directly after dark on the night of 8/9th October.
   Front tape about 50 yards behind the posts held by the Outpost Company - Approx: from V.26.c.65. to D.2.a.33. on which the first wave formed up.
   Second tape - 300 yards in rear of first tape - from approx: V.26.c.21. to D.2.a.80 - on which second wave formed up.

   Battalion Headquarters were at WINCHESTER FARM and Aid post at HUNTER FARM.

2.   Three hours before Zero, the whole Battalion was in position on the tapes.
   First line of first wave extended along the front tape, remainder of Battalion were in section columns in depth.
   About half an hour before Zero, enemy shelled WINCHESTER Line fairly heavily but this fell just behind second wave and only four casualties occurred.

3. ZERO - 5-20 A.M.
   First wave got away well with the barrage, followed at about 300 yards by second wave.

(1)

Enemy at once

Enemy at once opened M.G. fire all along the line, especially from shell holes in front of 2 MEBUS about V.26.d.46., redoubt about V.26.d.55.70, and trench running from D.2.b.86. to D.2.b.72.

Enemy's barrage fell well behind second wave.

(a) **First wave** - "B" Company cleared the Cemetery which was held by snipers and a machine gun team which was wiped out. They met with considerable opposition from machine guns in shell holes just in front of the two MEBUS about V.26.d.46. These were assaulted, the enemy surrendering when we got close up to them - about 30 prisoners and three M.G's being taken. A German Officer who appeared to be trying to rally his men was observed to be killed by them.

Estimated casualties of "B" Company in their attack -
1 Officer (2/Lt. E.D.WARREN)
45 other ranks.

"A" Company advanced in close touch with "B" Company's right, and met with considerable opposition from trench running from D.2.b.66. to D.2.b.72.

Lieut.POOLE (Coy. Commander) and 2/Lieut.TOWNSEND were wounded during the advance.

The right platoons entered the trench where they were later joined by part of "C" Company. They bombed up it towards the 7th Worcesters, capturing 20 prisoners and 4 machine guns - a good many more prisoners being taken by the 7th Worcesters. This party was commanded by Sergts. WILCOX & COURTIER.

The left platoons with some of the 7th Worcesters who had got over to them, advanced against VACHER FARM (which could not be recognised on the ground). They suffered considerable casualties and it is not very clear what happened here.

2/Lieut.SOUTHGATE with part of a platoon, kept touch with "B" Company on his left and eventually formed a post between BURNS HOUSE and VACHER.

Estimated loss of "A" Company in the attack -
2 Officers (Lt.A.G.POOLE & 2/Lt.W.C.TOWNSEND).
59 other ranks.

(b) **Second wave** - Owing to the strong opposition which the first wave encountered and the heavy state of the ground, the Second wave got close up to the first wave when they reached the BURNS - VACHER road, and they pushed through first wave in order to keep up to the barrage.

"D" Company on the left assisted "B" Company in capturing the 2 MEBUS and then advanced against the redoubt about V.26.d.55.70. This was strongly held by Machine Guns, which continued firing until our men were close up to them, when enemy came out of the redoubt with their hands up, also surrendering 4 machine guns.

"C" Company - The front line of "C" Company under 2/Lieut.B.A.TOUSSAUD, advanced in conjunction with "D" Company on their left through VACHER FARM, but the second line under 2/Lieut.A.S.HILL appear to have lost direction and to have gone too far to their right. 2/Lieut.HILL was killed early in the advance and Capt.TITLEY who was also with them, was missing until three days after, when he was brought in by the 9th Division and died of wounds in hospital. It is thought that they reached a point about 200 yards N.E. of BURNS HOUSE - VACHER Road.

Estimated losses of "C" Company in the attack -
2 Officers (Capt.R.G.TITLEY & 2/Lt.A.S.HILL).
56 other ranks.

OPERATION ORDERS NO. 42.
by
Lt.Col.H.St.G.Schomberg, Comdg. 1/5th Bn. Gloucestershire R.

Ref. Sheet 36C S.W., LENS II &
various sketch maps issued.

1. **RELIEF.** The Battalion will be relieved in the line today, 25th instant by the 1/7th Bn. Worcestershire Regiment.

2. **GUIDES.**
   "D" Coy. will send 5 guides (1 per platoon)) To be at junction
   & 1 for Coy. Hdqrs.-) PEGGIE-TEDDIE
   "C" Coy. will send 5 guides (1 per platoon)) Trench at
   & 1 for Coy. Hdqrs.-) 5-45 pm.

   "B" Coy. will send 5 guides (1 per platoon)) To be at
   & 1 for Coy. Hdqrs.-) junction DORIS-
   "A" Coy. will send 5 guides (1 per platoon)) HAYTER Trench
   & 1 for Coy. Hdqrs.-) at 6-15 pm.

3. **DISPOSITIONS.**
   "D" Coy. will be relieved by "A" Coy. 1/7th Worcs.
   "C" Coy.   "   "   "   "   "B" Coy.   "   "
   "B" Coy.   "   "   "   "   "D" Coy.   "   "
   "A" Coy.   "   "   "   "   "C" Coy.   "   "

4. **LEWIS GUNS & MESS STORES.**
   A limber for "D" Coy. will be at "D" Coy. ration dump at 8 pm. A limber for "C" Coy. will be at "C" Coy. ration dump at 8 pm. A limber for "A" Coy. will be at B.H.Q. at 9 pm. A limber for "B" Coy. will be at B.H.Q. at 9 pm. A limber for Hdqrs. will be at B.H.Q. at 7 pm.
   Lewis Guns and Mess Stores will be loaded as troops pass. 1 Lewis Gunner and 1 Officers' batman will accompany each Company limber, and 1 representative from Headquarters, the Headquarters limber. In the event of the limbers not being up when the first troops pass the respective dumps, the stores and Lewis Guns will be dumped, guarded, and loaded when limbers arrive.

5. **ROUTE.** On relief, the Battalion will proceed by road to CELLAR Camp, NEUVILLE St.VAAST. Route from B.H.Q. : HAYTER TRENCH - LENS ARRAS Road - FOLIE FARM Road (S.29.a.) - NEUVILLE St.VAAST. Officer i/c Headquarters Details will arrange for 2 Battalion Runners to be posted at convenient places to guide outgoing troops.

6. **COMPLETION OF RELIEF** to be notified by wiring the word THOMAS.

7. **ADVANCE PARTY.** 2/Lieut.A.H.WATTS, 1 other rank per Company and one from Battalion Headquarters will report at B.H.Q. at 3 pm., and will be proceeding to CELLAR Camp in advance and take over from the 1/6th Bn. Worcestershire Regiment.

8. **RETURNS.** Receipts for all trench stores etc. handed over is to be obtained and forwarded to B.H.Q. on the morning of the 26th. A duplicate copy of what is to be handed over will be sent to B.H.Q. by noon today.

9. **TEDDIE TRENCH.** There is to be no movement overland along the course of this trench during the daytime.

Lieut. & A/Adjt.,
25/10/17. for O.C. 1/5th Bn. Gloucestershire Regt.

Copies :- 1 - 4 Companies 5 & 6 War Diary
          7 Q.M.   8 T.O.
          9 1/7th Bn. Worc. Regt.

"D" Company - Having captured the redoubt, "D" Company were subjected to a heavy M.G. cross fire from OXFORD HOUSES. The 4th Gloucesters on our left had been unable to take this strong point and were apparently held up. Capt.J.A.FLETCHER was therefore obliged to form a defensive flank to his left before attempting any further advance. He threw out posts as far left as V.26.b.25.00, from which point he afterwards obtained touch with the 4th Gloucesters.

The two platoons of "C" Company under 2/Lieut.TUSSAUD and 2/Lieut.SOUTHGATE'S platoon, gained touch from HUNS HOUSE to the mixed force of "A" & "C" Companies under Sergts.COURTIER & WILCOX on the right who were in close touch with the 7th Worcesters on their right.

4. 3-20 P.M. - COUNTER-ATTACK.
Enemy were observed in Artillery formation about BANFF HOUSE and a line of skirmishers was observed about V.27.a.84. Lewis Guns and rifle fire was opened on them, and they withdrew. They made two further attempts to advance and were on both occasions driven back by our fire. The barrage which had been called for, fell at 3-40 pm and must have had good effect. No further movement was observed.

5. Our line on the night of the 9/10th October ran as follows :-
V.26.b.25.00 - V.26.d.57. - V.26.d.75.85 -
V.27.c.60. where touch was found with the
7th Worcesters.
Posts along the line were held and consolidated.

<u>Captures</u> :- About 70 prisoners & 12 Machine Guns.

<u>Casualties</u> - 242.

Lieut. Col.,
Comdg. 1/6th Bn. Gloucestershire Regiment.

www.ingramcontent.com/pod-product-compliance
Lightning Source LLC
Chambersburg PA
CBHW08085230426
43662CB00013B/2114